Putting on a Show

Putting on a Show

Theater for Young People

Kathleen McDonnell

Second
Story
Press

Library and Archives Canada Cataloguing in Publication

McDonnell, Kathleen, 1947-
Putting on a show; theater for young people / Kathleen McDonnell.

ISBN 1-896764-89-4

1. Children's plays, Canadian (English)
2. Theater--Juvenile literature. I. Title.

PS8575.D669T54 2004   jC812'.54   C2004-905268-3

First published in the USA in 2005

Edited by Pamela Delaney

Cover design by Counterpunch/Peter Ross
Cover art by Brad Harley

Text design by Lancaster Reid Creative
www.lancasterreid.com

Printed and bound in Canada

Second Story Press gratefully acknowledges the support of the Ontario Arts Council and the Canada Council for the Arts for our publishing program. We acknowledge the financial support of the Government of Canada through the Book Publishing Industry Development Program, and the Government of Ontario through the Ontario Media Development Corporation's Ontario Book Initiative.

ONTARIO ARTS COUNCIL
CONSEIL DES ARTS DE L'ONTARIO

The Canada Council | Le Conseil des Arts
for the Arts | du Canada

Published by
Second Story Press
720 Bathurst Street, Suite 301
Toronto, ON
M5S 2R4
www.secondstorypress.on.ca

The author's web site: www.kathleenmcdonnell.com

Acknowledgements

I've had the good fortune to work on these plays with Michel Lefebvre, Annie Szamosi and Pierre Tetrault — excellent directors and wonderful collaborators, not to mention very good friends.

I also want to thank the following people:

Phyllis Cohen, another good friend and a gifted composer

The casts, designers, composers and stage crew for the productions of *Loon Boy*, *Ezzie's Emerald*, and *The Seven Ravens*

Ron Chambers and the University of Lethbridge drama students who took part in the workshop of *Foundlings* in 2001

Anne Barber and Brad Harley of Shadowland Theatre — neighbors, colleagues and friends

Janna Smith at Youtheatre, Montreal

David Powell of Puppetmongers, Toronto

Pamela Delaney at Postscript Productions, Stratford, Ontario

Kim Selody and Leslie Francombe at Carousel Players, St. Catharines, Ontario

Laura McCurdy, Corina Eberle and Margie Wolfe at Second Story Press

Putting on a Show
Theater for Young People

Table of Contents

David Powell, courtesy of Puppetmongers

Introduction

For kids, there's nothing more exciting than putting on a show! I remember the great flurry of activity when my kids and their friends would announce, "We're putting on a show. You have to come see it!" A show time would be announced. The fold-up puppet theater would be trundled out of the closet. Small slips of paper would be cut up into tickets. The show would begin as the kids crouched down inside the puppet theater to provide the characters' voices, which were often drowned out by their uncontrollable giggles.

As they grew older, the kids dispensed with the puppet theater and raided the dress-up box for costumes so they could act out the parts themselves. Sometimes they wrote original songs for their shows, sometimes whole scripts. And sometimes the build-up to the big show was so intense, they didn't have much energy left for the show itself.

These shows were a lot like their usual pretend-play, but with an important difference: the kids weren't just playing for their own enjoyment — they were performing for us, their audience. From a very young age they had figured out that these three ingredients are all you really need to put on a show: A story, performers, and an audience.

Real life, real time, real space

The essence of theater is make-believe. From a high-tech Disney extravaganza to a local theater production to a puppet show in someone's living room — all theater is simply a version of "let's pretend." But in theater it's not only the performers who pretend; the audience has to pretend too. The name for this phenomenon among theater people is the "willing suspension of disbelief." The phrase is a bit of a mouthful, but what it means is that although the members of the audience know perfectly well that the events unfolding on stage aren't "real," they willingly put this rational knowledge aside and enter into the make-believe world of

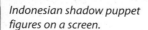

Indonesian shadow puppet figures on a screen.

the play. As an audience, when we take our seats in the theater we make a collective decision to go along for the ride. By suspending disbelief, we allow ourselves to experience the same emotions and sensations we'd feel if the events in the play were real. Because that's what theater is for: To expand our horizons, to take us places we can't — or don't want — to go in real life.

Movies and TV shows are also forms of make-believe. But watching a play is a very different kind of experience from watching movies and television. The term "theater" encompasses many different forms, from scripted plays to mime to opera. But the one thing that that all forms of theater share, and that distinguishes them from film and other forms of entertainment, is that they are performed live. A play is not a filmed or videotaped record of what a group of actors did weeks or months ago. It's happening right now, in real time and space. This creates an air of unpredictability and even danger that doesn't exist in film and television. In theater, things can and do go wrong: Actors forget their lines or miss a cue; a prop breaks or a costume rips. When these things happen, the actors and stage crew simply improvise a solution to the problem right there on the spot, and go on with the show. More often than not, the audience is not even aware that something went wrong. This quality of immediacy, of "aliveness," is one of the things that makes the experience of watching theater so special.

There's another important difference between film and theater: Although we also suspend our disbelief when we watch stories on film, the illusion looks much more real to us. This is especially true nowadays, with the hyper-realism of special effects and CGI (computer-generated imagery) in blockbuster fantasies like *The Lord of the Rings* and disaster movies like *The Day After Tomorrow*. Some people worry that these ever-more-lifelike special effects in movies may be spoiling the experience of live theater for audiences. But in my view, the low-tech, pure quality of live theater is precisely what makes it unique and exciting. Theater draws upon an audience's imagination in a whole different way from film and television. The illusion is right there for us to see through, yet we accept it. We embrace the world as the play presents it to us. In theater we have to use our imagination to fill in the blanks. We, the audience, actually become willing participants in creating the illusion. It's a special kind of magic that only live theater can provide.

Four thousand years and counting: A short history of theater

Humans have been putting on shows for a long time. The world's earliest recorded dramatic production took place in Egypt somewhere around the year 2000 B.C. A stone tablet found on the banks of the Nile contains an account of a performance of a play about the death and resurrection of the god Osiris. In the beginning

Medieval traveling players arrive to perform in a town square.

theater served a religious function in society. It grew out of rituals and ceremonies that provided ways for people to communicate with the spirit world. These rituals took place at seasonal festivals and included music, chanting and ceremonial dances.

Theater also grew out of storytelling, the ancient practice of reciting the myths and tales that were part of a culture's common heritage. Telling these stories aloud was the main way in which the myths were transmitted from one generation to the next. One of the oldest examples of this tradition is the *Mahabharata*, an epic cycle of tales from India that recount the intervention of the Hindu god Krishna in a centuries-long feud between two royal families. Storytelling is still important in theater today. Some contemporary plays are monologues, consisting of a single actor speaking directly to the audience, sometimes playing multiple roles.

Smithsonian Magazine

Large puppets depict characters from the Indian epic Mahabharata.

We think of words as the very basis of theater, but words were not nearly as important in the theater of the ancient world as they are today. There are other ways of telling stories, such as chanting, dance and music, techniques that were (and still are) prominent in the theatrical traditions of Africa and India. Masks were widely used in ancient theater because they heightened the sense of ritual and helped the performers submerge their own personalities in the characters they portrayed. The theater of Japan and China makes extensive use of masks.

Puppetry has also played an important role in theater history. We think of puppets as children's toys, but puppetry is at the heart of theatrical traditions all over the world. In Japan a style of theater known as *bunraku* employs half-life-size figures in which the puppeteers are plainly visible. Puppets have been used in India for centuries to tell stories from the *Mahabharata*. The earliest evidence of puppets in the Americas is the Hopi tribe's Great Serpent drama, in which giant snake figures were manipulated with strings. One of the oldest forms of puppetry uses two-dimensional figures that cast shadows on a screen lit from behind. This technique, known as shadow puppetry, goes back to prehistoric times and is part of the theatrical traditions of many countries including Indonesia, Cambodia, Thailand, Egypt and Turkey.

Japanese bunraku *puppets.*

These ancient forms of theater still flourish in many parts of the world today. Sicily has a vibrant tradition of marionettes or puppets-on-strings. *Wayang kulit*, or "shadow theater," is widely performed throughout Indonesia. And modern-day troupes like Canada's Shadowland Theatre continue the old crafts, using masks and shadow puppets in new ways.

The type of theater we're most familiar with today developed around the fifth century B.C. in Greece. The Greeks presented their plays on stages in enormous outdoor amphitheaters, and the ruins of many of these ancient structures are still around today. Their plays were likely the first ones to be written down specifically as scripts and known to be the work of individual authors. Most of the plays that have come down to us from ancient Greece were written by the three great dramatists of the era: Aeschylus, Sophocles and Euripides.

The earliest Greek plays consisted of chants recited by a group of actors wearing masks, known collectively as the Chorus. According to legend, an actor by the name of Thespis decided to step out of the Chorus and play one of the characters in the story. This legend is the source of the word "thespian," a traditional term for actor. It was Aeschylus who came up with the idea of adding a second actor, and later, Sophocles and Euripides added even more. Their innovations allowed the characters to interact with one another rather than just speak to the Chorus, and this created many more possibilities for dramatic conflict. Their plays also marked the birth of what people in the theater call the "fourth wall," an imaginary barrier at the front of the stage that allows the actors to behave as if the audience was not there.

Aeschylus, Sophocles and Euripides all wrote tragedies — intense, serious plays about the gods, fate and human suffering. These tragedies were a mainstay of Greek life and continued to serve the high moral and religious purposes expected of theater. But another type of play, comedy, didn't have to confine itself to the old myths and religious themes, and in fact dared to poke fun at these things. The great comic playwright of ancient Greece was Aristophanes. His plays combined broad farce with sharp political satire, and they were wildly popular with audiences. The plays of Aristophanes, as well as those of Aeschylus, Sophocles and Euripides, are still performed today, more than two thousand years later.

As theater developed over the next few centuries, it took many forms. In medieval Europe, troupes of traveling players pulled their carts into village squares and performed shows on top of them. These mystery and morality plays harked back to the earlier religious purpose of theater, and drew their stories exclusively from the Christian Bible. Another type of traveling show was the Mummers' Play, in which players in masks and costumes would go into people's homes and perform for money and food at festive times of the year. Mumming groups in parts of Britain and Newfoundland still carry on the tradition today. A form of theater known as *Commedia dell'Arte* sprung up in Renaissance Italy and became popular across Europe. These *Commedia* plays drew on familiar satirical storylines and used an array of stock characters wearing ornate costumes and masks. By the time of William Shakespeare, in sixteenth-century England, theater became largely separated from its ancient roots in religion and ritual, and looked much like the kind of theater we're familiar with today: A form of entertainment that people turn to for stories and experiences that take them out of their everyday lives.

From page to stage

Every play begins life as a spark in the mind of the writer or playwright. It is the playwright's job to come up with a story and characters, then set it all down on paper in the form of a script. Play scripts are written in a particular format consisting of dialogue

— the words spoken by the characters — and stage directions, which are usually in italics and indicate the characters' actions. Even a primarily visual show with little or no dialogue, like a mime or shadow puppet play, starts with a script or written outline.

Many plays use original stories and characters, but sometimes the playwright draws on an existing story — perhaps a novel, folk tale or incident from history — and adapts it to the stage. Later in this book, you'll find two different adaptations of a Brothers Grimm fairy tale, "The Seven Ravens." Playwriting is a very concentrated, disciplined form that usually requires a lot of rewriting. It's not at all unusual for a play to go through several rewrites, or drafts, before it is ready to be produced.

An Indonesian shadow puppet, seen from behind the screen.

David Powell, courtesy of Puppetmongers

Once the play is written, the playwright seeks out someone — an individual or a theater company — to produce the play. It's the producer's job to provide the money and space necessary to put on the show, and to hire the various creative personnel who will make it happen. The first and most important person to be hired is the director, who will ultimately be responsible for all creative decisions — casting as well as the overall look and feel of the production. The director is the one who can step back and envision the production as a whole. In a sense, the director stands in for the audience — even before there is an audience.

Directors give their own particular shape and interpretation to a show by the creative choices they make — the actors they cast, the designers they choose, and the way they work with all the various artistic personnel. Some directors might emphasize the comic elements of a given script, while others opt for a more serious approach. When you see the same script staged by two different directors, the result can be two very different experiences. Shakespeare's plays are probably the best-known example of this. Because they are performed so frequently, the challenge for a director is to find something new and unfamiliar, to come up with a fresh approach to the play. One common tactic is to set the plays in different time periods. For example, in 2003 I saw a production of *The Taming of the Shrew* at Canada's Stratford Festival. It was set in the wild west, complete with gun-toting cowboys twirling lassos.

The director's work starts well before the play goes into rehearsal, with auditions, casting decisions and consultations with the set designer and other artists. With a new play that has not been performed before, the director often works with the playwright on revisions to the script. Once rehearsals begin, the director works with the actors, often six days a week, helping them explore their characters and, in theater jargon, "putting the show on its feet." As the opening of the play draws closer, the director's job becomes even more intense, with daily run-throughs, and the setting of light and sound cues. Yet when the play is finally performed, the audience is largely unaware of the work of the director and all the other people who work behind the scenes. It's the actors they see, enjoy and connect with.

A word about actors

Many people think acting is some mysterious, magical process, but in truth, anyone can act. We all do it naturally as children, when we pretend we're dogs or doctors or superheroes. Adults do a kind of acting every day, when we try to present ourselves in a certain light at work or in social situations. (Interestingly enough, we sometimes accuse people of "putting on a show" when we think they're behaving falsely.) But professional acting is a craft, something you have to work at. Of course, certain people have a natural talent for acting, but even the most gifted actors have to undergo training and practice their craft.

I often visit schools where my plays are being produced. After a show the actors frequently hold a question-and-answer session, and one of the questions that often comes up is, "Are you on any TV shows?" Sometimes the kids ask for autographs, which the actors graciously give.

It's great to be treated like a celebrity for a day, but the truth of the matter is that actors don't go into acting to become celebrities. They do it because they are good at it, and because they love the work. Acting may look easy but it is hard work and takes tremendous discipline. People who tour young-audience plays to schools have to be particularly dedicated. They often perform several shows a day in addition to loading equipment, putting up and taking down the set.

Forget being a star. Working actors will tell you that the real joy of acting comes from collaboration, from working together to create something that didn't exist before. Actors love bouncing off one another's energy in rehearsal and in performance. I love seeing what actors bring to the words I write.

I'll tell you about an incident from early in my playwriting career that made a big impression on me. The play had a scene set in a hospital cafeteria, in which a character gives a fairly long speech expressing anxiety about her gravely ill husband. Rehearsals were going well, but the speech itself was flat and uninteresting. The actor* playing the woman had just finished her lunch before rehearsal, and there was an empty brown paper bag sitting on the table beside her. As she went through the speech yet again, she picked up the paper bag and began to fold it. Suddenly the scene came alive. When it was finished, the director instructed her to work even more with the bag, trying to get the folds just right so that it looked perfect, almost unused. The more the character concentrated on folding the bag just right (all the while speaking her lines) the more clearly her actions conveyed her emotional state to the audience. It was the perfect piece of body language to express the character's loss of control, her fear that her husband might die.

Contemporary use of masks in Shadowland Theatre's 2000 production Right of Passage.

Lorne Fromer, courtesy of Shadowland Theatre

I could have written the action of folding the paper bag in the stage directions, but I decided against it. Many of the best plays have minimal stage directions, in order to give actors and directors the freedom to discover the possibilities in the text in their own way. Actions that come across as natural in one production can end up looking mechanical in another. In general, it's better to let directors and performers discover the physical actions that work for them, so that the play feels organic and alive to the audience.

---

* In case you're wondering why I don't use the word "actress" here: Although it is still used, these days most people in the profession prefer to use the term "actor" for both males and females, since it refers to the performer rather than his or her gender.

The people behind the scenes

Here are some of the other people who work behind the scenes to put on a show:

The set designer is the person who creates the space where the action of the play takes place. Theater sets can be elaborate or simple, realistic or abstract, depending on the type of play and the particular approach of the director. What is important is that the set design reflects a clear vision, and effectively conveys the world of the play to the audience.

The lighting designer creates the lighting plan for the play. Perhaps more than anything else, it is lighting that determines the mood of a particular scene, and changes in lighting are used to shift the tone at various points in a play.

I really don't have to tell you what a costume designer does. But designing costumes is not just a matter of putting clothes on the actors or creating faithful reproductions of the styles of a particular period. Like the set and lighting, the costumes should help convey the particular world of the play, and the director's vision of it.

In a small- or low-budget, amateur production, the above jobs might all be done by the same person. In large-scale, professional shows, the various designers often have assistants and crews of people working under their direction.

The stage manager has a pivotal role in putting on a show. During the rehearsal period the stage manager often functions as a kind of organizational assistant to the director, keeping track of the various creative decisions and changes to the script. But his or her role really kicks in once the play opens. Then the stage manager is in charge of setting the props, coordinating the lighting and other cues, and basically making sure the play runs smoothly, night after night, performance after performance.

The members of what is called the front-of-house staff are also important. They are responsible for selling tickets, publicizing the play, escorting audience members to their seats, and a host of other jobs.

Depending on the play, there are others who might be involved as part of the creative team. A musical will have not only a composer to create the score, but also a musical director to conduct it during the performance. A show with significant dance elements requires the involvement of a choreographer. For plays with fight scenes, a specialist in fight choreography is usually brought in to coach the actors in how to avoid getting hurt while making the fight look realistic.

You will find descriptions of other theater personnel, as well as definitions of some terms used in theater production, in the Glossary at the back of this book.

So you want to put on a show...

As you can see, putting on a full-scale production of a play is a major undertaking, requiring skills and resources. But theater isn't something that only professionals can do. Remember what I said earlier: All you really need to put on a show is a story,

Contemporary use of masks in Shadowland Theatre's 2000 production Right of Passage.

Lorne Fromer, courtesy of Shadowland Theatre

performers and an audience. That's the essence of theater, and, like my kids' puppet plays, it can happen anywhere — a living room, a classroom, a community center, even a public park. If you have a burning desire to be more than a spectator of theater, don't be intimidated by the prospect of putting on a show. You can do it.

First, you have to find a script you want to perform. Think about things like what kind of stories interest you, how big a cast you want. Check out what is available in your local library or bookstore.

Once you find a script, keep in mind that you don't have to go for a full production. You can opt for a reading of the play in front of an audience. At a play reading, the actors usually sit in a semicircle and read their lines with scripts in their hands, with one person — often the director — reading the stage directions. There is also what's called a staged reading, where the actors move around and use simple props, still reading from their scripts. A reading is no substitute for a production, but it can convey quite a bit of the flavor of the play without the arduous, time-consuming work of blocking, staging and memorizing lines.

If you're planning a reading or putting on the play in a classroom situation, go ahead and use the published version. But if you're going to mount a full-fledged production, you should first obtain permission from the playwright. Most published plays will have contact information for the author or agent on the title page. If you'll be charging admission to the play, you will probably be asked to pay a fee, known as a royalty, to the playwright. Royalties are the main way in which playwrights get paid for their work, and royalties for non-professional productions are usually very modest.*

Maybe you don't want to put on an existing play. Maybe what you really want to do is create an original play of your own. Go ahead and give it a try. What kind of play do you want to create? What story do you want to tell? Something close to your own life? Something realistic? Or with strong fantasy elements? You can tell any kind of story in a theatrical way.

If you decide to write an original play, you can go about it the way most playwrights do and construct it line by line, scene by scene, on a computer or using old-fashioned pen and paper. Or you could bring a group of people together to pool ideas and create a play. This process is known as collective creation, and there are many different ways of going about it. Maybe the whole group will brainstorm ideas and appoint one or two people to go off by themselves and do the actual writing. Or the group could come up with a general outline and work up scenes by improvisation. However you go about it, at some point you need to have something on paper — if not a detailed script, at least an outline.

You'll need to find a director, or choose someone from the group to serve in that capacity. Even if you want to work in a loose, collaborative way, it's important to have a leader who pulls the show together, who can step outside and see the process as a whole. Next, find a place to rehearse, make up a rehearsal schedule and stick to it. Get busy making or borrowing your props and costumes. Maybe you'll decide to use a technique like puppetry to depict some of your characters. You can make simple rod and hand puppets yourself, or consult books on puppetmaking for more challenging ideas.

Decide if you're going to put on a one-time show or a run of performances. Set a date, find a place to perform the play, and put out the word so you'll draw an audience. You'll worry that no one will come. You'll be terrified when they do come. That's life in the theater.

---

* See the copyright page of this book for information on professional and amateur production rights to the plays in this book.

There's no one way to go about putting on a show, no set of hard-and-fast rules to follow. It all depends on the type of play and whether you want a polished or a more rough-and-ready production. Remember that the best way to learn about putting on shows is to go and see live theater as often as you possibly can. Check out the professional and amateur theater companies in your community. See if any touring companies are coming to your area. Invite a troupe that specializes in theater for young audiences to put on a show in your school gym or community center.

Even if you don't have many opportunities to see live theater, you can do the next best thing and read plays in their published form.

More than words on a page

When you read a play, it's important to keep in mind that it's not meant to be complete in itself. Unlike novels and short stories, which we read silently to ourselves, plays are meant to be spoken aloud, to be performed in front of an audience. In a sense, the play you are reading isn't all there. What's missing is the presence of the actors — their physical actions, their inflections and body language, the space they inhabit and the relationships they have with one another. Words on a page can only give a partial sense of what any given play will be like when it is performed.

You can get some of this quality of live theater by reading plays out loud. It might feel a bit strange at first, but reading aloud is a very good way to get a feel for what actors do. Try different ways of saying the same line and see what happens. Imagine yourself doing different physical actions, or better yet, get up and actually do them. See how it feels and how it changes your understanding of the words on the page.

The plays in this book are written for audiences that span about the same age range as the characters in the plays. Little Dove in *The Seven Ravens* is seven years old, Ezzie of *Ezzie's Emerald* and Lucas from *Loon Boy* are both eleven, while the young people of ancient Greece in *Foundlings* are in their teens. Like much contemporary theater for young people, these plays deal with issues like self-esteem and conflicts with parents. But they do so in a decidedly non-realistic way, populated as they are by Greek gods, fairy godmothers and characters who morph into loons and ravens.

Young-audience plays are like modern-day versions of those medieval travelling shows I mentioned earlier. You're just as likely to see one in a school gym or a community center as in a conventional theater. This is for practical and financial reasons, but it's also true to the ancient roots of theater, which is why I love working in this genre. Seeing a show in a school auditorium, with a set, props and costumes that all have to be packed up into a van, is seeing theater at its purest. It proves how little you actually need to create an illusion.

LOON BOY

A stage play in one act

Written by Kathleen McDonnell

Eric Fleming Denison, courtesy of Carousel Players

LOON BOY

I have to admit it: I have a thing about loons. While swimming and canoeing in Northern Ontario, I've had many close encounters with loons over the years, and one of the main characters in my fantasy novel series The Notherland Journeys is a talking loon named Gavi (for *Gavia Immer*, the Latin name for the common loon).

Writing *Loon Boy* was the point at which this passion for loons began to take shape. I read all about the birds — their migration patterns, mating habits, how they raise their young. During my research I came across an article about a group dedicated to protecting loon habitat by encouraging the use of floating "nest-islands." This notion struck me as a kind of metaphor for the small ways in which humans can heal some of the damage that we inflict on nature and on each other. The nest-island became the central image of the play, the thing that bonds the troubled boy, Lucas, and his foster mother, Ruby, even after Lucas has vented his rage on Ruby's beloved loons.

In the production of *Loon Boy* the loons were depicted by large bird-puppets carried overhead by the actors. There was no attempt to hide the puppeteers, nor any pretense that the loons were "real." Although the audience could plainly see the actors manipulating the puppets, after a few moments they ceased to pay attention to them and "saw" only the loons.

Try staging a couple of scenes from *Loon Boy*, using something as simple as a pair of wings mounted on a rod to represent the loons. See for yourself how readily your audience accepts them as part of the story.

Lucas (Johnathan Wallsten) and Ruby (Bie Engelen), flanked by puppeteers Garry Lynch and Francisca Zentilli, from the 1998 production of Loon Boy.

LOON BOY

LOON BOY was first produced by Carousel Players, St. Catharines, Ontario, in 1993 with the following cast and crew:

LUCAS	Martin Moreau
RUBY	Julie Wildman
SUSAN	Denise Norman
PUPPETMEISTER	Lawrence Tan

Director: Pierre Tetrault
Designer: Jerrard Smith
Choreography: Robert More
Lighting: Ken Garrett
Stage Manager: Catherine deGrosbois

LOON BOY was the recipient of a Chalmers Canadian Play Award in the Theatre for Young Audiences category in 1994.

LOON BOY

A stage play in one act
Written by Kathleen McDonnell

Production Notes:

The playing space consists of areas representing the inside and outside of Ruby's cottage on a Northern Ontario lake. Also on the lake is a rock with several Native pictographs (rock drawings) where Ruby's loon nest-island will be anchored.

Cast of Characters:

>   LUCAS, age eleven
>   RUBY, a foster mother, mid-fifties or older
>   SUSAN, a social worker

Note: The actor playing SUSAN can double as a puppet manipulator

Puppet manipulators are also needed to control bird puppets depicting two adult loons, a baby loon and an eagle.

Eric Fleming Denison, courtesy of Carousel Players

Ruby shows Lucas the nest-island in the 1998 production of Loon Boy.

Scene 1

LUCAS, alone, is playing with a hand-held computer game. He is completely caught up in whatever he is playing and talks animatedly to himself. Soundscape suggests the slam-bang digital sound effects associated with popular computer combat-style games. This soundscape recurs throughout the play whenever LUCAS plays his game.

LUCAS :   Come on, man, keep going. Get that sucker. Let's put 'em away once and for all. Right, right, keep going. That's it, you got it, you got it! Keep it up, keep it… Whoa! It's ZAR! Where'd he come from? Come on, come on, don't lose it now, don't lose it! The arm! Go for the arm! Go, go, go, go… Yes! I did it! I'm at Level Four! Yes! Yes!

Scene 2

RUBY emerges from the house carrying the nest-island. As she inspects it with great care a loon is heard overhead. She looks up to see the male loon returning for the season, and she watches with joy as it makes its skittering landing across the surface of the lake. SUSAN enters, unseen by RUBY, who is still lost in contemplation of the loon.

SUSAN: Ruby?

RUBY: Susan! Good God! I didn't hear your car.

SUSAN: I parked at the head of the driveway. Didn't want to get stuck in all that mud.

RUBY :   It's been ages!

SUSAN: I've never come up in the spring before. Your road is absolutely bursting with gorgeous wildflowers.

RUBY :   I'm so excited. Look! One of our loons is back.

SUSAN: Right. I forgot what a loon-atic you are, Ruby.

RUBY :   Oh, stop. You're as bad as Alf. He teased me all last summer about how I missed fostering so much I had to use loons instead of kids.

SUSAN: Ruby, I'm so sorry about Alf. We all are.

RUBY :   First time I've come up without him. Wasn't sure I could bring myself to do it. But I couldn't bear the thought of missing a summer at the lake. *(shows Susan the nest-island)* And I've got to get this thing in the water before that loon starts poking around for nesting sites.

SUSAN: *(totally mystified as to what it is)* Oh.

RUBY: I just finished it this morning. Alf and I started putting it together last summer. Before he took sick. Mind you, the real trick is, you have to get the loons to actually build a nest on the thing. Oh, listen to me, running on about loons. How are things at the agency?

SUSAN: Oh, as always. Too many messed-up kids. Not enough places to put them.

RUBY: Well, I'm glad I don't have to worry about all that anymore. But you still haven't told me what brings you up here. Let me guess. You're doing a placement up here and you couldn't let the local office handle it, you just had to check it out first hand. Am I right?

SUSAN: Well, half right. I've been going out of my mind looking for a placement for this eleven-year-old kid. I managed to get Lucas on the list for a group home near here, but they say they won't have room for him for a couple of weeks.

RUBY: Eleven, eh? What kind of trouble's he in?

SUSAN: He's been running with this gang of older kids and they're major trouble — B&Es, muggings, you name it. They beat up this old lady right on the street a few days ago when she wouldn't give up her purse. Lucas wasn't involved; he just watched. But we've got to get him away from that bunch. So, Ruby…

RUBY: Hmm?

SUSAN: We were thinking that just maybe you would consider…

RUBY: No, no! Noooooo. Stop right there.

SUSAN: I know what you're going to say, Ruby. But this is strictly short-term and…

RUBY: I said I was retiring and I meant it.

SUSAN: I know, Ruby, I know. But we're desperate to get this kid out of Toronto, and, to be honest … with Alf gone, I thought maybe you could use the money.

RUBY: We never gave a damn about the money before.

SUSAN: Of course not. But you're on your own now. You've got to be practical. I don't imagine Alf's pension goes all that far.

RUBY: I don't know, Susan. I'd like to help you out, I really would. But fostering was something Alf and I did as a team. Without him, I … Oh, come on. There must be someplace else you can send the boy.

SUSAN: I might be able to stick him with the Atlees for a while…

RUBY : You're not still using those people?

SUSAN: Sometimes, when there's nobody else.

RUBY : After what those foster kids said was going on in that house? I wouldn't trust the Atlees with my dog, much less an eleven-year-old kid.

SUSAN: None of that was ever proven, Ruby. And you know some of those kids are pathological liars. Anyway, what else can I do?

RUBY : Nothing. Except come up here and twist my arm.

SUSAN: Oh, Ruby, the last thing I want to do is put pressure on you. Lord knows how many times you and Alf came through for us all these years. They just don't make 'em like you two anymore.

RUBY : Right. Flattery will get you everywhere. When do you want to bring him up?

SUSAN: You mean that, Ruby? Oh, you're a peach!

RUBY : I'm crazy, that's what I am. What am I going to do with an eleven-year-old out here?

SUSAN: Look, you won't have any problem keeping him amused. He's addicted to one of those little computer games. Plays it morning, noon and night. What say I bring him the day after tomorrow? Right after the lunch?

RUBY : Fine. And for how long?

SUSAN: Oh, it shouldn't be more than … six weeks at the very most.

RUBY : Six weeks? You said two a minute ago!

SUSAN: It depends on when space comes up at the group home.

RUBY : I should have my head examined.

SUSAN: I'll take him off your hands as soon as I possibly can, Ruby. I promise you. I should get going.

RUBY : Come all this way and you won't even stay for coffee?

SUSAN: I really should get back to the city. When I bring him up on Thursday, okay.

RUBY : Fine, Susan. See you then.

SUSAN: Bye, Ruby. And thanks again!

SUSAN exits.

Scene 3

SUSAN and LUCAS arrive at Ruby's. SUSAN carries a bag containing Lucas' things. RUBY goes to greet them. LUCAS, totally absorbed in his computer game, ignores them both.

LUCAS:	C'mon! Go for the gun!
RUBY :	Susan! You finally made it.
SUSAN:	We got held up in traffic.
RUBY :	Here, let me take that bag. So this is Lucas.
SUSAN:	Lucas, come and meet Mrs. Laughlin. *(he ignores her)* Lucas? *(going over to him)* Lucas, put that thing down a minute, please.

Susan tries to take the game out of his hands.

LUCAS:	Hey!
SUSAN:	I asked you to put it down for a minute.
LUCAS:	You messed up my game!
SUSAN:	I want you to come and meet Mrs. Laughlin.
LUCAS:	I don't have to!

LUCAS stomps off by himself.

SUSAN :	Told you he was a tough customer.
RUBY:	*(going over to LUCAS and unfazed as he pointedly ignores her)* Why don't you take a walk around the place, Lucas? Go down the shore a ways. You might see some leopard frogs. They're just past the tadpole stage and they've been croaking up a storm the past few days. Later I'll take you out in the canoe. I've got a little job for both of us. Okay? *(getting no response, she goes back to SUSAN)* So. What's his story?
SUSAN :	Oh, you've heard it all before. Doesn't know his father. Mother lives in Kirkland Lake. She was only sixteen when she had him.
LUCAS:	Okay, now he's toast…
RUBY:	How come he's not living with her?
SUSAN :	She had this boyfriend. Real sweetheart of a guy. When Lucas was four they brought him into Sick Kids Hospital with a broken shoulder and bruises over half his body. Tried to tell the doctors he had a fall. Typical. The cops knew it was the boyfriend, but they couldn't get the mother to testify against him.

LUCAS:	C'mon! Blow him away!
SUSAN:	We took Lucas into care and found a family to adopt him. But, it just didn't work out. He's been in and out of foster homes ever since.
RUBY:	Doesn't matter how many times you see it, does it? Still makes you mad as hell. Want that coffee now?
SUSAN:	*(shaking her head)* I thought we'd make it up here earlier. I promised my kids I'd be home for supper. Here. *(hands her a brown envelope)* More notes on the sad saga of Lucas, if you can stand to read them. Lucas?
LUCAS:	*(ignores her)* Yes! Got him!
SUSAN:	I have to go now. I'll come back for a visit in a week or two. Okay? *(no response, she turns back to RUBY)* I'll give you a call in a day or two, see how things are going. I hope this is okay with you, Ruby.
RUBY:	Don't worry about me. I can handle this one.
SUSAN:	Take care, Ruby.

SUSAN exits. RUBY goes and gets the nest-island.

RUBY:	Well, Lucas. All set for our canoe ride?
LUCAS:	No, thanks.
RUBY:	I said I had a job for the two of us. Remember?
LUCAS:	I'll just stay here.
RUBY:	Come on. It'll be fun. We might see one of the loons.
LUCAS:	I said I'll just stay here!
RUBY:	Sorry, Lucas. I can't leave you here by yourself.

RUBY walks over and hands him a lifejacket.

LUCAS:	I have to wear this?
RUBY:	Absolutely.
LUCAS:	Why?
RUBY:	So you don't fall in and drown yourself.
LUCAS:	I'll look like a geek with that thing on!
RUBY:	*(putting on her own)* Then I guess we'll both have to look like geeks. Lucky we don't have much of an audience out here.

RUBY holds out the lifejacket, until LUCAS reluctantly takes it and puts it on.

RUBY: I don't suppose you've ever been in a canoe before. Now watch how I get in. *(stepping into the canoe)* See? Keep your weight in the centre. That'll keep it steady. Now you try.

LUCAS: *(looking down nervously, lurching into the wobbly canoe)* Ahhh!

RUBY: It's okay. Just sit down slowly. That's it. *(picking up the nest-island)* Here. Hold this for me a second.

LUCAS: What is it?

RUBY: Something the loons will build their nest on. At least I hope they will.

LUCAS shrugs, mystified by Ruby's explanation. RUBY gets in the stern and pushes off with the paddle. They paddle across to the pictograph rock, where the male loon appears. RUBY takes the nest-island from LUCAS and lowers it into the water close to the shore.

RUBY: There. I think that's just about far enough.

RUBY tosses a rock tired to a rope into the water.

LUCAS: *(still mystified)* What's that for?

RUBY: The rock? Oh, to anchor the nest-island, so it'll stay put.

A loon call overhead announces the arrival of a second loon.

RUBY: Look, Lucas! The female's arrived!

The two loons do a brief but spectacular courtship display. RUBY and LUCAS watch, then paddle back to the shore.

Scene 4

RUBY and LUCAS are in the house.

LUCAS: I told you the battery's run out!

RUBY: I heard you, Lucas. And I said we'll pick one up tomorrow.

LUCAS: I can't wait till then!

RUBY: I'm getting dinner. I can't just drop everything and run into town for a battery.

LUCAS: I'll go myself.

RUBY: It's a long walk.

LUCAS: I'll hitch a ride.

RUBY:	Not many cars on this road, especially after dark. Which is what it'll be on your way back. Look, Lucas. I can see how important your game is to you. We'll go pick up a battery first thing in the morning. I promise. Now, why don't you put on the TV?
LUCAS:	Yeah, right. Two lousy stations. What am I supposed to watch? "Sesame Street"?

LUCAS storms out of the house.

| LUCAS: | Stupid old bag. I'd like to pound her out. |

LUCAS stands looking at the blank screen on his computer game for a moment, then flings the game in frustration.

Scene 5

A day or two later. RUBY is in the house. LUCAS is outside, playing his game.

RUBY:	Lucas?
LUCAS:	Rats! Can't get it!
RUBY:	Lucas? *(by now familiar with this behavior, she walks over to him.)* I'm talking to you, Lucas.

RUBY puts her hand over the screen.

LUCAS:	*(whipping it away from her)* What?
RUBY:	I want you to take this bucket and dump it in the compost.
LUCAS:	Why should I?
RUBY:	Because there's work to be done around here, that's why.

LUCAS ignores her; goes on playing.

RUBY:	Do it, Lucas. Now.
LUCAS:	I don't have to.

RUBY grabs the game away from LUCAS. He lunges at her.

LUCAS:	That's mine. Give it back!
RUBY:	Not until you do what I asked you to.

LUCAS makes a move to hit her. RUBY blocks it and holds his arm tightly. He wrests himself free and runs a short distance away.

LUCAS:	Touch me again and I'll report you as a child abuser!
RUBY:	You go right ahead and do that, mister. There's work that has to be done, and as long as you're living here you're going to do your share. Understand? *(pause)* Look, Lucas. We're stuck with one another for the next little while. What do you say we try and get along?
LUCAS:	What about my game?
RUBY:	You'll get it back when you do what I asked you to do.

LUCAS sullenly picks up the bucket and starts walking. RUBY, satisfied, goes back inside. LUCAS notices a frog in the grass and starts to stalk it, slamming his hand down on it several times as it tries to hop away. After a time RUBY comes outside again. LUCAS hears her, picks up the bucket again and starts walking.

RUBY:	Lucas? Could you also take….? *(looking down in the grass, noticing the frog)* What….? This frog can't move. Poor thing looks like one of its legs is broken. Lucas? Do you know anything about this?
LUCAS:	Me? No. Why should I?
RUBY:	Are you sure?
LUCAS:	I said no.
RUBY:	How did this happen, then?
LUCAS:	How should I know? What's the big deal? It's just a stupid frog.
RUBY:	It's a living creature, Lucas. How would you like it if someone hurt you for no reason? How would it make you feel? *(picks up a rock and lifts it over the frog)*
LUCAS:	What're you doing?
RUBY:	Finishing what you started. *(she smashes the rock down on the frog's head)*
LUCAS:	You're killing it!
RUBY:	That leg won't heal. The poor thing'll just starve to death. This is quicker and kinder, believe me.
LUCAS:	Whoa. You are crazy!
RUBY:	If I ever catch you harming another creature on this lake there'll be hell to pay, Lucas! Understand?
LUCAS:	You are completely insane!

LUCAS runs off.

Scene 6

Several days later. LUCAS is playing his game while RUBY looks out over the lake with binoculars.

LUCAS:	Yes! Yes!
RUBY:	Hallelujah!
LUCAS:	I did it! I'm at Level Five!
RUBY:	She's on the nest-island, Lucas. I think she's laid an egg!

RUBY pulls LUCAS toward the canoe.

LUCAS:	Where're we going?
RUBY:	I've got to go see for myself. I'll bet there's an egg in there.
LUCAS:	*(muttering, putting on his lifejacket)* This is nuts.

They get into the canoe and push off.

LUCAS:	How come you don't use the motorboat? It's faster.
RUBY:	The motor's been down since last summer. I still haven't gotten around to getting it fixed. Anyway, it's too noisy. Scares the poor loons out of their wits.
LUCAS:	They're the ones who give me the creeps. Wailing all night.
RUBY:	*(straining to see the nest-island)* Yep. There's an egg under there, all right. Can't tell if there's one or two. They don't always lay a second.
LUCAS:	Hey, look.

The second loon swims toward the nest-island. The first loon gets off and swims away, as the second loon wriggles onto the nest.

RUBY:	They're doing a shift change.
LUCAS:	Huh?
RUBY:	They take turns keeping the egg warm. The mother's come to do her shift.
LUCAS:	How can you tell that's the mother?
RUBY:	She's a bit smaller. You can tell when you see them both together.
LUCAS:	I thought sitting on eggs was the mother's job.

RUBY:	Loons are a pretty enlightened species, Lucas. Loon fathers help with incubating the eggs and raising the chicks, too. And when loons choose a mate, they stay together for their whole lives.
LUCAS:	Let's get up closer.
RUBY:	Better not. We might scare her away.
LUCAS:	She wouldn't go away and leave the egg alone?
RUBY:	If she got frightened, sure. She'd probably swim away from the nest.
LUCAS:	How can she do that? She should stay there and protect it.
RUBY:	Well, Lucas, if somebody bigger and stronger comes after it, there's not a whole lot she can do. At least here no animals can get at it. Like raccoons - they're the worst. They steal eggs all the time.
LUCAS:	Why don't you just shoot them?
RUBY:	Who?
LUCAS:	The raccoons. If they steal eggs, you should just shoot 'em.
RUBY:	No, Lucas. It's not like that. The raccoons aren't doing anything wrong. It's normal for animals to prey on one another. I guess I want to give the loons a bit more of a fighting chance, that's all. When Alf and I bought this place there were always loons on the lake. Then for some reason they stopped coming — maybe because of all the boats disturbing their nests. Last year Alf came across an article about floating nest-islands for loons, and he got all hepped up about building one. I'll bet he's looking down on that egg with a big grin on his face right now.
LUCAS:	What happened to him?
RUBY:	Alf? Oh, he died last year. Just before Christmas.
LUCAS:	That's too bad. I mean, I'm sorry for you.
RUBY:	Thank you.
LUCAS:	Must get kind of lonesome up here, all by yourself.
RUBY:	Yes, it does sometimes. We should be getting back.

RUBY starts paddling. LUCAS suddenly stands up in the canoe.

LUCAS:	Hey! Hey!

The mother loon swims off the nest. The canoe becomes unstable.

RUBY:	Lucas, sit down! *(slowly steadies the canoe)* What are you doing? You almost tipped the canoe!
LUCAS:	I can't believe she did it.
RUBY:	What?
LUCAS:	She left the nest. I wanted to scare her, to see if she'd leave the nest like you said. *(calling to the mother loon)* Some mother you are!
RUBY:	*(shaking her head)* Lucas.

They paddle back to shore.

Scene 7

Later that evening, in the house. RUBY cleans up from supper while LUCAS plays his game.

RUBY:	Almost time to get ready for bed, Lucas.
LUCAS:	Not yet. I just started Level Five. It's really cool.
RUBY:	*(looking over his shoulder)* Just what is it you kids see in these things, anyway?
LUCAS:	See this little guy here? I'm playing him, and this mean ugly monster called ZAR keeps trying to kill me, so I have to get past him and each time I do, I get to another level. But it keeps getting harder and harder to get by ZAR. There, that's one of his creepy little gnomes. You gotta kill it, see?
RUBY:	It's awfully violent.
LUCAS:	That's the fun of it. Anyway, they're bad guys. It's okay to kill bad guys. Oops, missed one!
RUBY:	What's that noise mean?
LUCAS:	Just that I have to go back to the start of Level Five again. Here, you try.
RUBY:	Me? Nooo. I'm useless around computers.
LUCAS:	It's easy. I'll take it back to Level One.
RUBY:	It's getting late, Lucas…
LUCAS:	Come on, just try it. To start the action you press this. Then you move the little guy along like this. See?

RUBY: *(taking the game)* All right. Just for a minute …

LUCAS: Okay, now keep moving him along. There, there, get that weapon! No, no. You're letting it get away. Rats! Keep going, you can try for the next one. Wait! There's another one of those gnomes. You gotta go around him, you don't have a weapon, you … Ahhhh!

RUBY: What happened?

LUCAS: You're dead.

RUBY: I'm dead? That's what happens when you lose? You die?

LUCAS: Sure. Either you kill them first or they kill you. That's the way it works.

RUBY: Well, so much for my computer game career. Now get ready for bed.

LUCAS: Sorry. I guess I shouldn't have said that.

RUBY: Said what?

LUCAS: About… being dead. I didn't mean to remind you, or anything.

RUBY: Remind me? Oh, you mean about Alf? It's all right, Lucas. I know you didn't mean anything by it.

LUCAS: Will I still be here when that egg hatches?

RUBY: Hmm. Let's see. It'll probably be another three weeks, but Susan did say a month or so. Why? Would you like to be here?

LUCAS: Yeah. Yeah, I really would.

RUBY: I don't see why not. I'll call Susan tomorrow and let her know. That way you can be the first to see the chick swimming around on the mother's back. Now go to bed.

LUCAS: I still think she's a lousy mother. Leaving her nest like that.

RUBY: You're really bothered by that, aren't you?

LUCAS: She should stay and protect it. That's what mothers are supposed to do.

RUBY: What about your own mother, Lucas?

LUCAS: What about her?

RUBY: Do you think about her?

LUCAS shakes his head.

RUBY: If you ever want to talk about her…

LUCAS:	What's to talk about? I never see her. She could be dead for all I care.
RUBY:	Lucas…
LUCAS:	I want to go to sleep now.

LUCAS turns away from her.

Scene 8

The next day. RUBY is showing LUCAS how to use a pair of binoculars.

RUBY:	Now, to focus, just turn this knob here. Slowly, slowly, till everything becomes nice and sharp. Are things getting clearer?
LUCAS:	Yeah. Hey, neat. I can see the mother loon on the nest, like she was right up close. She's swimming around right near the nest. Hey, she just dove under.
RUBY:	Probably trying to catch a fish for lunch. Look up and down the far shore a bit. See what else catches your eye.
LUCAS:	What's that big opening in the woods over there?
RUBY:	An old logging road. Years ago they cut a path through the woods so they could haul lumber out. It's pretty overgrown now, but it goes right out to the highway. I walked all the way into town once along that road. Took me five hours.
LUCAS:	You walked for five hours? Whoa!
RUBY:	People have been known to do such things and survive, Lucas. Look! Over there. Check out that bird. See if you can catch it in the binoculars. Use the focus knob the way I showed you.
LUCAS:	Got it.
RUBY:	What's it like?
LUCAS:	Big. Kinda brownish.
RUBY:	Hmm. Could be an eagle. Got to watch those guys. They're nest-raiders.
LUCAS:	It's starting to circle over the nest. And I don't see the mother anywhere.
RUBY:	Keep an eye on it, Lucas. I'll be right back. I thought I heard a car motor.

LUCAS moves closer to the nest-island, still absorbed in looking through the binoculars.
SUSAN enters but he doesn't see her. During RUBY and SUSAN's exchange, an eagle
appears and swoops down near the nest-island a few times, as LUCAS watches fearfully.

RUBY: Susan!

SUSAN: Surprise! She strikes without warning again.

RUBY: You must've read my mind. I tried to call you this morning, but they
           said you'd be out for the day.

SUSAN: Well, I've got news for you and I just had to deliver it in person. I got a
           call from the group home this morning and guess what? A space has
           come up for Lucas. Somebody moved out earlier than expected.

RUBY: Oh.

SUSAN   He can move in right away. Isn't that great?

RUBY: You mean, you want to take him there right now?

SUSAN: Oh, no rush. You can take your time getting his things together and I'll
           finally get that cup of coffee you owe me.

RUBY: Well, I'm… flabbergasted.

SUSAN: Told you I'd take him off your hands soon as I could. Ruby, what's the
           matter? I thought you'd be glad.

RUBY: Something's come up. That's why I tried to get hold of you this
           morning.

SUSAN: What?

LUCAS: *(to the eagle)* Hey!

RUBY: Lucas has gotten very attached to the loons. He's all excited about the
           nest, and last night he asked me if he could stay here till the egg
           hatches.

SUSAN: When will that be?

RUBY: Another three weeks.

SUSAN: Three weeks? I can't leave him here that long, Ruby. They won't hold
           the space.

RUBY: You told me I'd have him six weeks. That's why I told him he could stay
           to see the chick. I didn't think there'd be any problem.

SUSAN: I'm sorry, Ruby. How could I know a space would come up this soon?

RUBY: Look, I know this loon thing doesn't sound like a big deal, but it is to Lucas. It's like he's finally found a way to connect with something outside himself, and I want to see it through with him.

SUSAN: I see what you're saying, Ruby, but I don't know what I can do. This group home has kids clamoring to get in. If we don't take the space some other agency will snatch it up, and we'll be right back at square one.

RUBY: That kid gets shunted around like a piece of furniture.

LUCAS: Go on, beat it!

SUSAN: You think I enjoy this? Trying to find homes for kids absolutely nobody wants? You of all people should know what I'm up against.

RUBY: I'm sorry.

SUSAN: Look, the group home's not that far from here. I can try to swing it so he can come back for a visit when the egg hatches.

RUBY: Right. The group home staff are really going to have time to go driving Lucas around the countryside.

SUSAN: I'll bring him myself if I have to. It's the best I can do, Ruby.

RUBY: Listen, he hasn't noticed you're here. I want you to go now and come back tomorrow.

SUSAN: Tomorrow? Ruby, I drove all the way up here …

RUBY: I need time to break it to him. If you slip up the driveway now he won't see you.

SUSAN: Ruby, I …

LUCAS: You're history, scumbag. Kapow!

RUBY: Let me handle this my way, Susan. If that boy's well-being means anything you can wait one more day.

SUSAN: All right. I really am sorry about all this.

RUBY: I know.

The eagle flies away.

SUSAN: I'll see you tomorrow around noon.

RUBY: Fine. Good-bye, Susan.

SUSAN exits. LUCAS rushes back to RUBY.

LUCAS: Mrs. Laughlin! You were right! It was an eagle and it… Hey, that looks like Mrs. Petrillo's car up at the end of the driveway. Wha…? She's pulling away.

RUBY: Oh, she was just checking in.

LUCAS: Funny she didn't talk to me. They usually do. "How do you like your placement, Lucas?" As if they cared.

RUBY: She was in a bit of a hurry to get back to the city.

LUCAS: It was just like you said! The eagle was after the egg. It came swooping down really low over the nest, and the mother swam away. But I scared it off! Really, I did! It flew away!

RUBY: Good work, Lucas.

LUCAS: I bet it thought I was a hunter. *(pretending to shoot)* Ka-pow! Ka-pow!

LUCAS races offstage down the shore again, as RUBY watches.

Scene 9

That night. RUBY and LUCAS are in the house. LUCAS is playing his game as usual.

LUCAS: At this level ZAR keeps popping new arms every time I shoot one off. Rats! Did it again! I swear I'll never get past this one.

RUBY: You'll have to finish up soon, Lucas.

LUCAS: You haven't complained about the noise once tonight. How come?

RUBY: Guess my mind's been somewhere else. Lucas, there's something we need to talk about. Mrs. Petrillo … had some news for me today.

LUCAS: Yeah? What?

RUBY: A space has come up for you in the group home.

LUCAS: Oh.

RUBY: Mrs. Petrillo just got the call this morning. Someone moved out earlier than expected. So it looks like you'll finally be able to settle down in one place for a while. Mrs. Petrillo is thrilled. She thinks it's a really good place.

LUCAS: Yeah, they always say that. When do I go?

RUBY: Tomorrow. But I'm going to arrange for you to…

LUCAS: Tomorrow?

RUBY: I told her all about the egg, Lucas. She knows how important it is for
             you to be here, and she promised she'd arrange for you to come back
             and visit around that time.

LUCAS: Visit? You said I could stay!

RUBY: I know I did, Lucas. I didn't think there'd be any problem. Neither Mrs.
             Petrillo nor I had any idea a space would come open this soon.

LUCAS: But you said!

RUBY: Honey, if it were up to me, I'd…

LUCAS: I thought you were different but you're just like all the others.

RUBY: Lucas, listen to me…

LUCAS: You do it for the money, just like everybody else. You're probably
             ticked off they're taking me early so you won't make as much!

RUBY: That's not true…

LUCAS: *(running out of the house)* I'm just as glad anyway. This place sucks. It's
             boring. I hate it!

RUBY: Lucas, come back here!

LUCAS races over to the canoe, gets in and pushes off with the paddle.

RUBY: What do you think you're doing?

He paddles away quickly. RUBY races along the shore, unable to stop him.

RUBY: Get back here this minute! It's getting dark! Lucas!

LUCAS: I'll get you. I'll show you.

*LUCAS arrives at the nest-island and practically slams the canoe right into it. The mother
loon, fearful, slides off the nest and swims away, giving a tremulous distress call. He pokes
the egg with the paddle.*

LUCAS: See? I can do anything I want to it! You can't stop me! Aren't you
             going to do something? Aren't you gonna protect it? Huh? Stupid
             bird!

He slams the paddle down on the egg. A loud crack!

LUCAS: Who cares? Stupid bird.

RUBY's voice is heard in the distance.

RUBY: Lucas! Lucas!

LUCAS paddles to the far shore near the nest-island and gets out of the canoe.

LUCAS: I'll find that road she was talking about. When it gets light. I'll hitch a ride to Toronto and see if I can find my buddies. Too dark now. She can't come after me. She's got no motor. Yeah. I'll find that road. Five hours. Man, it's dark. I can't even see the house anymore. Why can't I see her light? Getting cold.

LUCAS holds himself, starting to shiver. After a few moments he lies down on the ground and curls up in a fetal position. Lights fade to black.

Scene 10

Lucas' dream-journey begins. The actions in this sequence can be carried out by the bird puppets, possibly in combination with shadow images on a rear screen. The soundscape and lighting should make clear that everything is occurring in dream-time, not real time.

LUCAS appears to wake up. He gets up, a bit groggy, and looks around.

LUCAS: Hey, where am I…? Oh, yeah. Yeah. The egg. Oh man, she's gonna kill me when she finds out…

He suddenly spies the loon egg in the nest. Miraculously, it is whole again, undamaged, looking, if anything, larger and more perfect than before.

LUCAS: Whoa, man! I don't believe it! I could have sworn I…

RUBY suddenly appears. She seems to be carrying something behind her back. She glares at LUCAS.

LUCAS: Ruby? Oh, wow, am I ever glad to see you! I was really…

RUBY: How would you like it if somebody hurt you for no reason? How would it make you feel?

LUCAS: Huh?

RUBY walks past him toward the egg. She pulls out the object from behind her back — a rock — and lifts it over her head, as she did with the frog earlier in the play.

LUCAS: Ruby? Ruby! *(rushing toward her)* What are you doing?

RUBY: Finishing what you started.

LUCAS: No, you can't do that!

RUBY: This is quicker and kinder, believe me.

LUCAS manages to stop RUBY just in time. They struggle over the rock. He finally manages to wrest it from her.

LUCAS: What is with you?

RUBY suddenly starts to giggle.

RUBY: Oh, come on. It's just a game.

LUCAS: Yeah? You had me scared for a minute there.

RUBY: You know that game. It's called: Kill them before they kill you! *(starts to laugh uproariously)* It's fun!

LUCAS: You are completely insane!

RUBY exits, still laughing.

LUCAS hears a small cracking sound behind him and whirls around.

LUCAS: What's that?

LUCAS watches in awe as small cracks begin to appear in the egg.

LUCAS: Wow. That's wicked!

More and more cracks appear, until the sides of the egg fall away, revealing a loon chick. The chick fluffs its down.

LUCAS: Hey, little guy. Hey.

The loon mother appears. The loon chick slides onto her back, and they start swimming away.

LUCAS: That is so cool! It's just like she said.

The mother loon dives for a fish. She brings it up to the surface and feeds it to the loon chick.

LUCAS: Wow. You got quite an appetite, little guy.

The mother loon begins flapping her wings along the surface of the water, preparing to take off. The loon chick flaps its wings in imitation.

LUCAS: See? She's trying to teach you to fly, little guy. That's right. Keep working at it. You'll get it.

The mother loon takes off and flies away.

LUCAS: Hey! Where you going? Wait up! You can't just leave him here! He's too little! He doesn't know how to fly yet! *(to the chick)* Don't worry, little guy. She probably just went to a lake where there's better fishing. I bet your dad's on his way right now. Loon fathers do that, you know. They help take care of the babies…

An eagle appears in the sky overhead.

LUCAS: Uh-oh.

The eagle begins to swoop down toward the loon chick, who manages to dive under the water to escape.

LUCAS: He can't stay down that long. I don't know what to do. I gotta get some help!

The loon chick surfaces. The eagle makes another terrifying swoop toward it as it dives under the surface again.

LUCAS: Oh, no. No. Somebody! Help! Help!

LUCAS begins to run, screaming. He sees a woman standing with her back to him. He calls to her.

LUCAS: Mom? Mommy? Is that you? You gotta help me, Mom. That eagle's after the loon chick and…

The woman turns around and faces LUCAS. It's SUSAN.

LUCAS: Oh, it's you. Sorry, Mrs. Petrillo, I…

SUSAN: You think I enjoy this? Trying to find a home for a kid nobody wants?

LUCAS: Please, Mrs. Petrillo! You gotta help me! I gotta save the baby loon! Please…

SUSAN: *(walking away, ignoring him)* What can I do about it? There's too many messed-up kids and not enough places to put them. Just too many messed-up kids.

SUSAN exits. LUCAS races back and starts attacking the eagle with imaginary weapons.

LUCAS: You're history, scumbag!

Finally the eagle flies away.

LUCAS: He's gone. We did it. We're okay, little guy. See? We showed him. We're okay. We can do it. I'll take care of you, little guy. I won't leave you.

After a moment, the eagle returns.

LUCAS: *(clutching the baby loon protectively)* It's okay, little guy. Don't worry. I won't let him get you.

The eagle dive-bombs the two of them again. There is a struggle. LUCAS fights hard, but the eagle snatches the baby loon away from him and takes off again.

LUCAS: *(trying to chase after the eagle)* No! No!

RUBY enters, carrying something.

LUCAS: Ruby! Ruby, you gotta help me! An eagle came and…

He stops suddenly, realizing she is holding the baby loon.

RUBY: If somebody bigger and stronger comes after you, there's not a whole lot you can do about it.

RUBY hands LUCAS the baby loon. It falls limp in his arms.

LUCAS: *(sobbing)* No! No!

Scene 11

LUCAS suddenly wakes up to find RUBY standing over him.

LUCAS: Ruby!

RUBY: Lucas! Thank God.

LUCAS: Man, am I glad to see you.

RUBY: You scared the living daylights out of me!

LUCAS: How'd you get here?

RUBY: I figured you might head for that old logging road, so I drove to the highway and hiked in. Why did you do this, Lucas?

LUCAS: I don't know. I'm sorry.

RUBY: Come on. We'll talk about it back at the house. I'll get a neighbor to drive me out to the car later. Where's the paddle? *(spying it)* Oh.

RUBY walks over to get the paddle and notices the nest.

RUBY: Oh my God! What happened? Oh, it's all… Look, Lucas, the egg! It's… Oh no! *(she is momentarily overcome with tears)* What could have done this? I just don't understand it. I've never seen an eagle tear up an egg like this… Was it like this last night, Lucas?

LUCAS: I don't know. I didn't look.

RUBY notices something on the paddle.

RUBY:	What's this, LUCAS?
LUCAS:	What?
RUBY:	Why is there blood on this paddle?
LUCAS:	I don't know.
RUBY:	What happened here, Lucas? Who did that to the egg?
LUCAS:	I said I don't know!
RUBY:	I want the truth, Lucas. Who did this? Who did this?
LUCAS:	It was an accident…
RUBY:	You little… *(raises her hand to hit him, stops herself)* You wanted to hurt me? You wanted to get back at me? Well, you sure found the way to do it. Mrs. Petrillo's coming for you today and you know what? I'm glad. That's it. I'm fed up. I wash my hands of you. *(turns away and heads for the canoe)*
LUCAS:	I said it was an accident! If you just give me a chance to explain…

LUCAS runs after RUBY and tries to grab her arm. She shakes him off violently.

| RUBY: | You are one sick boy, Lucas. You're so twisted up inside, they should lock you up and throw away the key right now! |
| LUCAS: | I'm sorry! *(calling after her)* I said I'm sorry! |

Scene 12

Some weeks later. SUSAN and LUCAS arrive at RUBY's. As they approach the house, LUCAS stops, hangs back.

SUSAN:	Lucas? Is something wrong?
LUCAS:	She hates me. She's gonna kill me.
SUSAN:	No, she's not.
LUCAS:	She's gonna chew me out. That's what all this is for, isn't it?
SUSAN:	Look, Lucas. Ruby wouldn't have had me drive all the way up here just so she could yell at you.
LUCAS:	Then why?
SUSAN:	I don't know. Honestly. She said there was something really important she wanted to show you. That's all I know.

LUCAS:	You're sure she wants to see me?
SUSAN:	I'm sure. Now, come on. It's going to be okay.

RUBY appears, goes to greet them.

RUBY:	Hello there.
SUSAN:	Hey, what gives? You told me that road would dry up like a bone once summer came. It's muddy as ever!
RUBY:	Oh, you just need better tires on that thing. Hello, Lucas.
LUCAS:	Hi.
RUBY:	How've you been?
LUCAS:	Okay.
RUBY:	How's it going at the group home?
LUCAS:	Okay.
SUSAN:	They tell me he's turning into quite the gardener. He got put in charge of the tomato patch.
LUCAS:	Yeah. That's what they do there. Gardening and stuff. They even got compost, like you.
RUBY:	You don't say.
SUSAN:	Well, I'll let you two visit for a while. Lucas, I'll pick you up in an hour or so, okay?
LUCAS:	Yeah, sure.
RUBY:	And there'll be coffee ready by then.
SUSAN:	Great. You're on.

SUSAN exits. Left alone, RUBY and LUCAS are awkward, a bit nervous.

RUBY:	So. Still playing your computer game?
LUCAS:	Nah. I got tired of it.
RUBY:	Oh, really?
LUCAS:	Yeah, battery ran down one day and I just didn't bother getting another one.
RUBY:	Dead battery, eh?
LUCAS:	Yeah.

They both smile at the memory of their earlier fight.

RUBY: Lucas, I owe you an apology.

LUCAS: Apology? What for? I'm the one who should be sorry.

RUBY: No matter what you did, I had no right to say the things I said to you. I was very angry, and very hurt. I'm sorry.

LUCAS: I think about it all the time, Ruby. I still don't know why I did it.

RUBY: It's all right, Lucas.

LUCAS: You don't hate me, do you?

RUBY: No.

RUBY puts her arms around LUCAS and he begins to cry.

LUCAS: I swear I'd give anything if I could bring it back.

RUBY: Let's go out in the canoe, Lucas. There's something I want you to see.

LUCAS wipes his eyes on his shirt and follows her into the canoe. They paddle to the nest-island.

LUCAS: Look, Ruby!

One of the loons is swimming with a baby on its back.

RUBY: It just hatched yesterday.

LUCAS: But how…? It couldn't have… I don't get it.

RUBY: The mother laid a second egg. When loons lose an egg early in the season, they usually try again. This time we got lucky. That nest-island worked like a charm.

LUCAS: Awesome!

RUBY: See, Lucas? Nature doesn't hold grudges. No matter what we do, she just keeps giving us another chance.

The baby loon slides off his mother's back.

LUCAS: Look! He's doin' it! He's swimming on his own.

RUBY: And look who else is coming.

The father loon appears and does a joyous display overhead. The mother loon flaps her wings, preparing to take off. The baby loon imitates her.

LUCAS: Go on, little guy. You can do it.

The mother loon takes off. The baby loon flaps harder, on the verge of lifting off.

LUCAS: That's it. Yes! Keep it up! You're doin' it.

Finally the baby loon takes off.

LUCAS: Way to go, little guy!

THE END

EZZIE'S EMERALD

A stage play in one act

Book and Lyrics by Kathleen McDonnell
Music by Phyllis Cohen

Brad Harley, Shadowland Theatre

EZZIE'S EMERALD

I adapted this play from my first children's book, about an overweight girl named Ezzie who performs an act of heroism. There's a moment in the book when Ezzie makes a wish on her emerald and has a fleeting glimpse of a fairy godmother. For the most part, the story stays in the realm of familiar, everyday reality. But when I revisited the story to rework it as a play, I decided to be bolder and make the fairy godmother a full-fledged character — the comically inept Ralda, who finally succeeds in winning her third-class Cosmic Emerald pin.

Ezzie's Emerald was my first attempt at creating a musical, working with composer Phyllis Cohen. I knew that the best musicals used songs as an integral part of telling the story, and that's what I set out to do with this play. The first song, "Anyone Else," expresses Ezzie's longing to be thin and popular. Later, on the playground, Shannon sings through the entire guest list for her sleepover, pointedly letting Ezzie know she's being excluded.

Phyllis Cohen's score is not included in this book. If you want to read sections of the play out loud or put it on at your school, feel free to recite the lyrics or improvise your own melodies to them. To obtain a copy of the score, please refer to the information regarding performance rights on the copyright page.

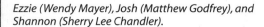

Ezzie (Wendy Mayer), Josh (Matthew Godfrey), and Shannon (Sherry Lee Chandler).

EZZIE'S EMERALD

EZZIE'S EMERALD was first produced by Carousel Players, St. Catharines, Ontario, in 1995 with the following cast and crew:

EZZIE	Wendy Mayer
RALDA	Donna Preising
SHANNON	Sherry Lee Chandler
JOSH	Matthew Godfrey
Director:	Pierre Tetrault
Composer:	Phyllis Cohen
Set Design:	Brad Harley and Anne Barber
Costume Design:	Monika Heredi
Musical Director:	Phyllis Cohen
Stage Manager:	Susan Casasanta

Musical numbers, in order, and their performers:

"Anyone Else" — Ezzie
"You Are Strange" — Josh and Ezzie
"Parties Are Great" — Shannon and Ezzie
"PFG" — Ralda and Ezzie
"Anyone Else" (reprise) — Ezzie
"KidsWorld" — Josh and Shannon
"You Are You" — Ralda and Ezzie
"What Do You Know?" — Ezzie and the company

Lyrics by Kathleen McDonnell
Music by Phyllis Cohen

EZZIE'S EMERALD

Book and Lyrics by Kathleen McDonnell
Music by Phyllis Cohen

Production Notes:

The set consists of two main areas at either end of the playing space. One is Ezzie's home — more specifically, the bathroom, with a sink and mirror. The other, larger area is the playground of Ezzie's school, where most of the action takes place. In between these two spaces is the route Ezzie takes to school, bounded at each end by bushes large enough to conceal both the dog and Ralda at different points in the play. There is also a small fenced-off area on this route where the dog is tied up, next door to which is Baby Nina's house.

Cast of Characters:

EZZIE, age eleven
RALDA, Ezzie's Personal Fairy Godmother, age indeterminate but more child than adult
JOSH, age eleven, Ezzie's childhood pal and classmate
SHANNON BARRY, age twelve, the best-looking, most popular girl in Ezzie's class

EZZIE'S MOTHER is heard only as a voice from offstage.
The BIG BOSS in Scene 1 is also represented only as an off-stage voice.
The DOG could be represented by a life-size puppet manipulated by one of the actors.
BABY NINA could be represented by a doll or puppet in a carriage, also manipulated by one of the actors.

Personal Fairy Godmother (PFG) played by Donna Preising in Ezzie's Emerald.

Scene 1

RALDA walks hesitantly onstage. The voice of the BIG BOSS — warmly authoritative, definitely female — is heard offstage.

RALDA: You … sent for me, ma'am?

BIG BOSS: Yes, Ralda. The senior FGs have been discussing your future.

RALDA: You have?

BIG BOSS: We think you've been hanging around in fourth class a bit too long. Don't you think it's time you got serious and went after your CEP3?

RALDA: My third-class CEP? I can't! I'm not ready!

BIG BOSS: We think you are.

RALDA: But what if I fail? The PFGs will all laugh at me.

BIG BOSS: Failure's an important part of the learning process.

RALDA: I knew you'd say something like that.

BIG BOSS: Don't worry, Ralda. I know you'll succeed at this assignment. She's been hand-picked for you. Her name is Esme. Get it? She's Esme, you're Ralda. Esmeral…

RALDA: Ralda! *(forced laugh)* Oh, I get it. What's her damage, I mean, problem?

BIG BOSS: At the moment, she doesn't like herself very much.

RALDA: I can relate to that.

BIG BOSS: Well, Ralda, you have your instructions. Goodbye and good luck.

RALDA: Wait! How will I find this Esme?

BIG BOSS: You'll find her. Just let yourself be drawn by the power of her wishes!

(Opening of "Anyone Else" comes up)

Scene 2

Ezzie is at the bathroom mirror.

EZZIE: *(sings)* I wish that I could be some other girl — not me
My hair would be long and straight
My body would be the perfect weight
And my complexion would be clear and clean
Like cover girls on *Seventeen*

But movie stars and models aren't like me
How beautiful I'd be
If only I weren't me.

Ezzie's mother's voice is heard from offstage.

MOTHER: Esme, stop dawdling in front of that mirror.

EZZIE: I've got a snarl.

MOTHER: If you wore your hair shorter you wouldn't get so many snarls.

EZZIE: I don't want short hair. I want mine really long, like Shannon Barry's.

MOTHER: Who's Shannon Barry?

EZZIE: Oh, only the best-looking, most popular girl in the school. She's always tossing her hair back and it looks totally wicked. *(tries tossing her own hair back)* Except when I do it. Mom? Remember those guys I was telling you about?

MOTHER: Which ones, honey?

EZZIE: You know. The ones who're always bugging me on the playground. They were at it again yesterday. "Hippo! Hippo!" I hate them.

MOTHER: Just ignore them, sweetheart. Pretend you don't hear them. If they see they can't get a rise out of you, they'll stop.

EZZIE: I've tried that. It doesn't work.

MOTHER: You know, if you could only lose a few pounds, Ezzie. It's a shame. You have such a pretty face…

EZZIE: Yeah, right.

MOTHER: You do. Now get a move on or you'll be late for school.

EZZIE: *(sings)* I wish that I could be more self-controlled than me
I'd stick to healthy, low-cal stuff
Stop eating when I'd had enough
No Mr. Bigs or Hostess chips
Just oranges, Trident, celery sticks
But every time I try, it's agony
How beautiful I'd be
If only I weren't… *(catching sight of her face in the mirror)*
Mirror, mirror on the wall
You're no help to me at all!
Make me gorgeous, make me glow
The star of my own TV show
My life is getting out of hand
I need some magic! Understand?

MOTHER:	Esme?
EZZIE:	I'm going!
MOTHER:	Don't forget your jacket.
EZZIE:	Do I have to?
MOTHER:	It's cool outside!
EZZIE:	Okay.

EZZIE:
Okay.
(sings) I wish you'd grant my plea for popularity
I'd be the best, tres hip, way cool
The Queen of my entire school!
I'd seize the playground for my court
So Shannon Barry, eat my shorts!
Though I know it's all some childish fantasy
I still wish I could be
Someone — anyone! — else, not me.

EZZIE puts on her jacket and leaves. RALDA pops up into the mirror, dressed in a gauzy fairy princess get-up, holding a wand with a garish green jewel on the end. She watches Ezzie depart, then speaks to the audience.

RALDA: Yes! The jacket! Now we're cooking with gas!

RALDA exits.

Scene 3

EZZIE grabs her jacket and book bag and starts off for school. On the way she passes BABY NINA sitting up in her carriage. As EZZIE talks to her, NINA makes gestures and gurgly baby sounds in response.

EZZIE: Hi, Nina! How are you today? Oh, you're so cute I could eat you right up! Where's your mommy? Oh, there she is, working in the garden. Hi, Mrs. DiCecco! Ohhh, what's this, Nina? *(picks a toy out of the carriage)* A brand new rubber ducky! *(squeezes it and it squeaks; NINA laughs)* Can you say "ducky," Nina? "Ducky"? *(squeezes it again, making NINA laugh)* You're so lucky, Nina. You just sit here in your carriage and play with your squeaky toys all day. Life's gonna be a lot more complicated when you get older, you know. You'll have school, and homework, and you'll have to do chores like sorting laundry…

JOSH appears down the street.

EZZIE: Hey, there goes my buddy, Josh. Me and him have known one other since we were babies just like you, Nina. Hey, Josh!

JOSH:	Hi, Ez.
EZZIE:	Wait up! Gotta go, Nina. See you after school. Bye!

EZZIE catches up with JOSH.

EZZIE:	I came up with the best idea for the story assignment! Listen to this: "The XY Files: a race of alien chromosomes try to take over the earth."
JOSH:	*(to audience)* Do you know this person? *(sings)* You are strange, you're weird, you're very bizarre, Ezzie Words could never convey how different you are When your brain starts churning out mental debris Some people think you're out of your tree Some people, maybe But not me
EZZIE:	Look who's talking! Your last story was "Duck Trek," starring Captain JeanLoon Picard! And you're the one who covered Mr. Frankish's desk with ghost gum last Hallowe'en!
JOSH:	Well, at least that was funny. Anyone who pulls the kind of pranks you do is in serious need of professional help. *(sings)* Do you remember the Barbie doll? You stuck it with pins and took off its head Then you planted that Barbie in your sister's bed She thought it was a voodoo doll and freaked, half dead!
EZZIE:	Ah, Josh, you're forgetting something. The voodoo Barbie was your idea.
JOSH:	Oh, right. *(sings)* You are strange, you're weird, you're very bizarre, Ezzie.
EZZIE:	*(sings)* You are strange, you're weird, you're very bizarre, Josh
BOTH:	*(sing)* Words could never convey how twisted you are With all of the ludicrous things that you do It's amazing they don't lock you up in a zoo But lucky for you I'm loony too!
JOSH:	Ezzie, don't mention the Barbie doll to the guys at school?
EZZIE:	What's it worth to you?
JOSH:	Come on, Ezzie. You can't betray your oldest friend!
EZZIE:	Oh fine. Your secret's safe with me. Race you the rest of the way to the playground!

They both start running. As she passes the fence EZZIE is startled as a DOG suddenly comes bounding toward her, barking ferociously. It is chained to the other side of the fence. EZZIE races away from the fence and the barking dies down.

EZZIE: God, I hate that dog! It has a cow every time anybody walks past here!

JOSH: I sure wouldn't want to be around if it ever got loose. My dad says a dog like that can take off your whole face in a matter of seconds. They're trained to do that!

EZZIE: Let's just get out of here. Come on!

EZZIE starts to run. JOSH starts to follow, then pulls up abruptly. He notices something on the ground, picks it up.

JOSH: Ez, wait up!

EZZIE: Huh?

JOSH: Something fell out of your pocket. *(hands it to her)*

EZZIE: I don't believe it.

JOSH: What?

EZZIE: My emerald! I looked all over for it last spring and it's been sitting in my jacket pocket all this time!

JOSH: Awesome. Let me see. Hmm. Doesn't look very shiny.

EZZIE: It's not supposed to be. It's a raw emerald. That's how they look when they come out of the ground. My Aunt Rue brought it back from South America. She says it's my power stone, 'cause my name comes from Esmeralda. That's Spanish for emerald.

JOSH: Cool.

EZZIE: 'Course I don't really believe it's magic or anything. I just think it's pretty.

They approach the playground. The sounds of running, shouting, general hubbub. SHANNON is standing in the middle of the playground, looking around impatiently.

EZZIE: Oh, rats!

JOSH: What?

EZZIE: I forgot I was supposed to get here early. I'm on playground duty all this week. With Shannon. Yuck!

JOSH: I think Shan's nice.

EZZIE: I can't stand how all the girls crowd around and do her bidding, like they're her slaves or something. And she's more obnoxious than ever, now that she supposedly got that modeling job.

JOSH: She sure is good-looking enough to be a model.

EZZIE: Since when do you care about how people look?

JOSH: Who says I care? I was just making a comment.

SHANNON catches sight of EZZIE and JOSH.

SHANNON: You're late, Ezzie. Playground monitors are supposed to be here by eight-fifteen.

EZZIE: I forgot.

SHANNON: No problem. You can make it up to me later. Hi, Josh. Hey, cool boots.

JOSH: Thanks, Shan.

SHANNON: Are they Docs?

JOSH: Well, not really.

EZZIE: They're obviously not Docs. The soles are way thinner.

SHANNON: They're nice-looking anyway. Personally, I don't believe in getting all hung up on labels. Excuse me. I have work to do. *(picks up a brightly-colored binder)*

JOSH: Guess I'll go shoot some baskets with the guys.

SHANNON: Bye, Josh.

EZZIE: *(whispering to JOSH as he goes)* "Nice boots, Josh…"

JOSH throws EZZIE a look of annoyance and goes offstage to another part of the playground. EZZIE looks over at SHANNON, who is writing in her notebook.

EZZIE: I thought we were both supposed to be monitors

SHANNON: You were late, remember? You owe me. Anyway, I've got to finish this guest list before the bell rings.

EZZIE: Guest list? For what?

SHANNON: Oh. Didn't you know? There's a sleep-over.

EZZIE: Sleep-over?

SHANNON: *(sings)* Saturday night, it's going to be totally rad
We'll eat ketchup chips, stay up all night, we'll all go hysterically mad.
It's my job to figure out who to invite…

EZZIE: *(sings)* I'm not doing anything Saturday night.

SHANNON: Yeah? That's really too bad.

SHANNON ignores EZZIE as she works on her guest list.

SHANNON: Parties are great
To contemplate
Plotting each girl who'll be a guest
It's so cool
Making the rule
Figuring out who will pass the test
And it's fun
Being the one
Who gets to say, "She's in," "She's out!"
May not be nice
But that's the price
That's what life is all about

It's not like I try to be mean
Or have a nasty streak
But if you let the whole school in
What's the point of having a clique?

It's really keen
Being the queen
Absolute leader of the crowd

And I love
Giving the shove
Saying, "Sorry, no geeks allowed"
How low they stoop
To get in the group
They practically bow down on their knees
It's like, wow!
They have a cow!
They actually beg: "Oh, choose me, please!"

It's hard to be the Queen of Mean

The big tarantula
But someone's got to do the job
And it might as well be moi!

Julie's got that new to-die-for jacket from the GAP
She'll be so glad to be asked, I could borrow it in a snap
But Kimberly I cannot stand, she's so obnoxious, such a flirt

But seeing as Julie's her best friend, if Kim's left out then she'll be hurt
Sarah? Nah. Courtney? Maybe. Anna, Kai, Rebecca, Sue…

EZZIE: *(sings)* Shan? I'd really like to come, if that's okay with you…

SHANNON: *(sings)* Gee, I'm sorry, Ezzie, if I'd only known before…
                   'Cause only sixteen girls can come, there's just no room for any more.

                   Hey, that was fun!
                   The list is done
                   Finished the whole thing in a flash
                   I can't wait
                   It'll be great
                   We're gonna have a wicked bash

SHANNON stands up and starts to rush away, then stops abruptly and speaks hurriedly to EZZIE.

SHANNON: Ezzie, will you take over pleeease? I have to go deliver the invites.
                   Thanks!

SHANNON exits. RALDA peers out from behind the bush at the edge of the playground, watching EZZIE.

EZZIE: *(sings)* Go away
                   I'll be okay
                   What makes you think that I need you?
                   I'll be all right
                   Come Saturday night
                   I've got better things to do
                   Though you think that you're hot stuff now
                   You're headed for a fall
                   'Cause my turn's coming really soon
                   And then I'll show you…

Suddenly boys' voices and laughter rise out of the playground hubbub.

VOICES: Hippo! Hippo! Hippo!

Ezzie's mother's voice is also heard in an offstage echo.

MOTHER: *(offstage)* Just ignore them, honey. Pretend you don't hear them.

VOICES: Hippo. Fat hippooooooo.

MOTHER: Just ignore them. Pretend you don't hear them. Just ignore them. Just
                   ignore them.

VOICES: HIIIIPPPPOOOOO! *(snorts, gales of laughter)*

Everything stops as the bell signals the start of school. JOSH comes back onstage and tries to rush past EZZIE on his way into school. She calls after him.

EZZIE:	Some friend you are!
JOSH:	What's with you?
EZZIE:	I hate people who make fun of you behind your back!
JOSH:	I don't know what you're talking about!
EZZIE:	I saw you with them. I saw you laughing!
JOSH:	I didn't do anything!

JOSH turns to go into school. EZZIE rushes up behind him.

EZZIE:	You did too! *(whacks him on the back of the head)*
JOSH:	Ow! That hurt! *(starts to cry)*

SHANNON comes bounding over.

SHANNON:	Ezzie! What are you doing?
EZZIE:	Nothing.
SHANNON:	I saw you hit Josh.
EZZIE:	Well, him and those others guys were…
SHANNON:	Playground monitors are supposed to stop fights, not start them. Remember? Are you okay, Josh?
JOSH:	*(pulling himself together, acting manly)* Yeah, yeah, I'm okay.
EZZIE:	I suppose you're gonna report me?
SHANNON:	I'm only doing my job.

The bell rings a second time. SHANNON and JOSH file into school. EZZIE lingers behind.

SHANNON:	*(to Josh, as they exit)* Honestly. Hitting people is so immature…
EZZIE:	Great. Now the principal's going to call my mom, and my mom's going to freak… *(in Shannon's direction)* OOOOhhh, I wish your beautiful, creamy complexion would turn to chili dog vomit!

EZZIE exits. RALDA comes out from behind the bush.

RALDA:	Okay. She finally found the emerald. That's good! Wishing somebody's face turns to chili dog vomit? That's not so good. We aren't supposed to do negative magic. It says so right in the CE third-class handbook. Now if I can just get her to make a good wish on the emerald we'll be away to the races. What about this outfit? Is it too much? Do you think I should try for something a little more … Oh, I don't know! *(exits)*

Scene 4

The bell signals the end of school. EZZIE and JOSH come out onto the playground. EZZIE tries to ignore him. He calls after her.

JOSH: You walking home?

EZZIE: I don't know.

JOSH: *(shrugs)* Okay. See ya.

EZZIE: I'm glad you and your buddies find me so funny!

JOSH: Ezzie, it's no big deal. They used to make fun of me all the time for being short. They're just kidding around.

EZZIE: It's not the same thing.

JOSH: Look, everybody gets razzed for something. That's the way school is. You can't get all upset about it.

EZZIE: Funny, I don't see anybody razzing Shannon.

JOSH: Well, she's … I don't know…

EZZIE: She's different?

JOSH: What have you got against her, anyway? She's nice if you get to know her…

EZZIE: Nice? Has she ever got you snowed.

JOSH: *(turning to go)* I'm going home. See you later.

EZZIE: *(singing after him)* Josh has a crush, Josh has a crush…

JOSH: Shut up, Ezzie.

EZZIE: Josh has a crush, Josh has a crush, Josh has a crush…

JOSH: I can see why Shan has all the friends and you don't!

JOSH exits. His comment shuts off EZZIE's taunts. She stands looking after him for a moment.

EZZIE: Wow. This day's just getting better and better. I know. I'll just take this wonderful magic emerald out of my pocket *(she does so)* and make a wish on it and my whole life will change and everything will be perfect. See, I'll close my eyes and wish for all the things I want, just like my weird Aunt Rue told me to. *(closes her eyes; as she speaks the sarcastic edge in her voice turns to real anger)* I wish those guys on the playground would leave me alone. I wish I was popular like Shannon. I wish I were queen of the playground and everybody would do exactly as I say. *(suddenly opening her eyes)* I don't believe I'm doing this.

EZZIE flings the emerald behind the bush and starts to rush away. Suddenly there's a loud poof! and a cloud of mist rises from behind the bush. EZZIE swirls around. There's RALDA, decked out in an even more outlandish getup than before. She still carries the emerald wand, however.

RALDA: Whoa!

EZZIE: Huh?

RALDA: Being visible is a whole different experience!

EZZIE: What?

RALDA: Oh, sorry. I forgot. You don't have a clue who I am.

EZZIE: Are you from that alternative school or something?

RALDA: No. I'm Ralda!

EZZIE: So?

RALDA: Ralda! Get it?

EZZIE: It's a weird name, but we got all kinds in this school.

RALDA: No, no, no, no, no. You're Esme. I'm Ralda. EsmeRalda. Don't you get it?

EZZIE: No!

RALDA: You called me. You made a wish on the emerald, and here I am. I'm your PFG.

EZZIE: Excuse me? My PFG?

RALDA: Personal Fairy Godmother!
            (sings) We haven't met before, we two
            But I've kept my eye on you
            Now I am here to lend a hand
            Your every wish is my command
            For service with a lifetime guarantee

            Call your friendly PFG!

EZZIE: Let me see if I have this right. You are my own Personal Fairy Godmother? *(RALDA nods)* And you've come in answer to the wish I made on the emerald? *(RALDA nods)* Why am I surprised? You look about what I'd expect to get for a Fairy Godmother.

RALDA: What, is it the clothes? They're all wrong, aren't they? I knew I should have stuck with the pink gown and the tiara!

EZZIE: Let's just say nobody's going to mistake you for Costume Ball Barbie.
(sings) To be a real, live Fairy Queen
One must be lovely and serene and wise and good, like Glinda
But look at you, you're just a kid, like me
No way you're a PFG.

RALDA: You're wrong!

EZZIE: Oh yeah? Well, prove it!

RALDA: I will! Give me a chance!
It's just…

EZZIE: Well, what?

RALDA: It's my first gig
I lack… experience.

EZZIE: Oh, great. Exactly what I need. A trainee!

RALDA: *(sings)* Just starting out is no disgrace
The Big Boss put me on your case
She said if I did well I'd win
My third-class Cosmic Emerald pin!
So listen up, you gotta let me be
Your one and only PFG

EZZIE: *(sings)* I once threw coins in wishing wells
Broke wishbones, chanted magic spells
But now I'm past that
It's really time I faced reality
I don't need a PFG

RALDA: *(sings)* But hold on, girl, it's no time to stop.
If we play this right, we'll both come out on top.
Now I know you wanna be the playground queen,
And get those guys to stop treating you mean.

EZZIE: How do you know that?

RALDA: I have ways, my dear.

EZZIE: I'm starting to believe you're not from here.
Can you really change the ways things are?

RALDA: *(sings)* I can do way more, I can make you a star!
Don't pass up this chance, it'd be so tragic
When all that you want can be yours by magic!
I'll do it all for you, just leave the rest to me
Your one and only PF…

EZZIE:	*(sings)* You're my PF…
RALDA:	*(sings)* I'm your PF…
EZZIE:	*(sings)* Be my PF…
RALDA:	I hereby declare by the power of the Great Cosmic Emerald that in the next twenty-four hours you, Esme Phelan, will be transformed into the most popular girl in school!
BOTH:	*(sing)* G!

RALDA brandishes the wand over EZZIE.

EZZIE:	Wow. I feel strange. Kind of tingly all over. I can't believe this is happening! Am I really going to be more popular than Shannon?
RALDA:	How about this? You will get more attention in one day than Shannon Barry gets in a whole year.
EZZIE:	Awesome! And will I get thin, too? Does this mean I can wear tight jeans?
RALDA:	Honey, you'll be better than thin.
EZZIE:	This is so great! This is so totally unbelievable! Oh, thank you, thank you. What did you say your name was again?
RALDA:	Ralda. Remember? EsmeRal…
EZZIE:	*(shaking her hand)* Ralda, right.
RALDA:	Oops. Time's up. I'm starting to feel a little tingly myself.
EZZIE:	Huh?
RALDA:	I gotta go. We PFGs can't afford to push this visibility thing too far.
EZZIE:	You're leaving? But … what happens now?
RALDA:	What do you mean? It all happens now. Just you wait!
EZZIE:	But … are you sure I don't have to do something first? Like, go through trials and stuff, the way they do in fairy tales?
RALDA:	Humans! Who can understand them? You offer them a free lunch and they insist on paying for it! You're not as smart as you look. Here! *(tosses the emerald at a startled EZZIE, who catches it)* Keep this with you all the time. You're going to need it. And don't let me catch you throwing it away again. You hear?

RALDA disappears in a poof.

Scene 5

EZZIE starts running home excitedly. Half way there she stops and holds up the emerald, still in her hand.

EZZIE: Is it true? Could this really be a magic stone? I swear it's even starting to look shinier… *(gazes into the stone)*
(sings) Mirror, mirror, can it be?
Is there magic just for me?
Can't believe that you'll come through
To make my secret dreams come true
The time has come and you know how
Give me a new life, starting…

EZZIE is suddenly interrupted by a loud growl.

EZZIE: What's that? *(looks down at her feet, notices the dog's broken chain hanging from the fence; the dog is nowhere to be seen)* The dog. It must have gotten loose somehow. I better go tell somebody before it…

EZZIE starts to run down the street but is interrupted by another loud growl. The DOG's shadow appears.

EZZIE: *(very quietly)* They say not to look at it. They say if you just ignore it and walk away quietly it'll…

The DOG barks loudly, followed immediately by a baby's cry.

EZZIE: Nina! Oh gosh. I can't leave her there. What do I do? There's nobody around! What do I do?

Slowly and deliberately, EZZIE starts walking toward Nina's carriage. The DOG makes more low growls and NINA starts to whimper.

EZZIE: Shhh, Nina…

Just before EZZIE reaches the carriage the DOG comes bounding toward them, snarling and barking. EZZIE screams and lunges for the carriage. She grabs NINA. The DOG is almost on top of them.

EZZIE: Mrs. DeCecco! Somebody! Help!

EZZIE holds on to NINA for dear life, screaming for help over the DOG barking and Nina's cries. Suddenly EZZIE turns to face the DOG, and the tenor of her voice changes.

EZZIE: No! Go on, get away. You hear me? I said get away!

The barking dies away.

Scene 6

Loud theme music suddenly intrudes, startling EZZIE. She looks dumbfounded as two ultra-hip media interviewers (JOSH and SHANNON) bound onstage, completely ignoring her as they race past.

JOSH:	Hi, I'm Lance.
SHANNON:	And I'm Erica.
JOSH:	And this is…
BOTH:	KidsWorld!
JOSH:	The show that brings you news about kids from around the world…
SHANNON:	And around the block!
JOSH:	Today our special guest is an eleven-year-old girl who performed the most incredible good deed right on her own street…
SHANNON:	Totally awesome…
JOSH:	She single-handedly fought off an attack by a vicious dog and saved an eighteen-month-old neighbor child from severe injury, perhaps even death…
SHANNON:	What this girl has done is, like, so brave, I mean, I could never do anything like that…
JOSH:	That's right, Erica. She's the youngest resident of this city ever to be awarded a Citation of Bravery, and we've got our own special surprise award for her as well. Will you welcome, please, Ezzie Phelan!

EZZIE walks forward in a daze, to fanfare and audience applause. She tries to respond to the interviewers' questions, but they don't give her a chance.

SHANNON:	*(sings)* Ezzie! What kind of dog was it, Ezzie?
JOSH:	*(sings)* Ezzie, were you scared?
SHANNON:	I'd've been!
SHANNON:	Hey, Ezzie, is it true you're the guest of honor at the sleepover?
JOSH:	The big sleepover?
BOTH:	The big one Saturday night!
SHANNON:	Ezzie Phelan, you're so pretty.
JOSH:	Ezzie Phelan, what a doll!

SHANNON:	Where'd you get those cool boots, Ezzie?
JOSH:	Ezzie Phelan, you got it all!
BOTH:	Ezzie Phelan, you're tres hip! How could we not have seen? Ezzie Phelan, be our playground queen! Though we know we are not worthy of you…
EZZIE:	That's true…
BOTH:	We bow to Ezzie, our ruler, now.

SHANNON places a large, gaudy crown on EZZIE's head.

EZZIE:	Now, by the power of the Great Cosmic Emerald, I do hereby declare myself the most popular girl in school!

All freeze as RALDA pops out from behind her bush.

RALDA:	Oh No! What have I done?

RALDA exits.

Scene 7

When the music stops, Ezzie's moment of triumph suddenly ends. It's like she's waking up from a dream. JOSH and SHANNON shed their hip disguises and become their ordinary playground selves. EZZIE sheepishly removes the Playground Queen crown from her head before they can see it, then runs over to JOSH.

EZZIE:	Josh! You won't believe what happened yesterday!
JOSH:	What?
EZZIE:	The dog got loose! I was walking by there after school! It was going right for Nina! I grabbed her just in time and chased it away!
JOSH:	You're kidding!
EZZIE:	No! I just stood there and looked him right in the eye, and I'm like, "Don't even think about it, pal." And he ran away, just like that!
JOSH:	Awesome!
SHANNON:	What's going on?
JOSH:	Ezzie saved a baby from this vicious dog in our neighborhood!
EZZIE:	You wanna know the most amazing part? Mrs. DeCecco called the cops, and they said they're going to put in my name at the mayor's

office for one of those bravery medals! I might even get my picture in the paper!

SHANNON: Hey, I know, Ezzie! Maybe they'll invite you on that KidsWorld show! You know the one where they interview kids who've done good deeds and junk?

EZZIE: You think they might?

JOSH: I know that show! It's on Saturday mornings. It's wicked!

EZZIE: You should've seen it, Josh, the dog was…

SHANNON: That girl, Erica? I was supposed to audition for her part.

JOSH: Whoa! Are you kidding? She's like a big star now. I saw her in this jeans ad on TV.

SHANNON: My agent says she's going to get me some commercials. She just sent out a whole bunch of my portfolio shots. I've got them in my bag. You want to see them?

JOSH: Yeah, sure.

EZZIE: It was barking like crazy, just like when you and me went by there yesterday morning! It was almost as close to me as you are, but I managed to grab Nina with one arm and…

EZZIE is interrupted by voices and laughter.

VOICES: Hey! No hippos allowed on the court. Hippo!

EZZIE: *(trying to ignore them)* I knew I couldn't outrun him carrying Nina like that, so I just turned and looked right at him…

VOICES: Hippo! Hippo! Hiiipppooo!

JOSH: Just don't pay any attention to them, Ez.

EZZIE: Fine for you to say. They're not doing it to you!

SHANNON: You coming, Josh? The bell's going to ring soon.

EZZIE: Why don't you help me?

JOSH: What can I do?

EZZIE: I don't know … Tell them to shut up!

JOSH: Tell them yourself!

EZZIE: They won't listen to me!

JOSH: What makes you think they'll listen to me?

EZZIE:	They're your friends!
JOSH:	But they… Look, Ezzie, I…
EZZIE:	Just forget it! Go! Get lost!

JOSH follows SHANNON offstage as EZZIE races off the playground.

EZZIE:	What's the use? Everything's exactly the same as it was before! *(takes out the emerald)* I can't believe I was so stupid! It's just an ugly little hunk of green stone! *(flings it away)*

RALDA suddenly pops up from behind the bush.

RALDA:	Ah, ah, ah! Remember what I told you? *(flings the emerald back to Ezzie, who catches it in spite of herself)*
EZZIE:	It's you! I can't believe you had the nerve to come back!
RALDA:	I had to.
EZZIE:	What, so you can use me to get another one of your stupid pins? Where is it, anyway?
RALDA:	My third-class Cosmic Emerald pin? I didn't get it.
EZZIE:	Why not? 'Cause your magic stinks? You don't have to tell me that.
RALDA:	Ezzie, look, I'm sorry. I kind of messed up.
EZZIE:	That's putting it mildly.
RALDA:	You were my first big assignment. I really wanted to do well. But I was trying so hard to make a good impression on the Big Boss that I got carried away. She sent me back to try to get it right this time.
EZZIE:	Wait a minute. You mean, you really can give me a different life?
RALDA:	No, Ezzie. That's where I went wrong. Nobody can become something they're not.
EZZIE:	I knew you'd say something like that! What's the point? I do something good, I'm the big hero for a day but it doesn't make one bit of difference to those jerks on the playground!
RALDA:	Don't let them get away with that stuff. Go back there and tell them off.
EZZIE:	I can't!
RALDA:	You've got to, Ezzie. You have to believe in yourself. It's not going to be easy. I know. It took me forever to work my way up to third-class level. Sometimes it feels like I'm just never going to get that pin.

EZZIE:	So this is what you call magic. Great.
RALDA:	Ezzie, there is another kind of magic. The true kind, the only kind that really works. It's what I should have used in the first place.
EZZIE:	Thanks, but I don't want any more of your so-called help.
RALDA:	Ezzie, please, let me try…
EZZIE:	Just go away, will you?
RALDA:	All right. I'll still be watching over you if you change your mind. *(starting to leave, pauses)* Whether you realize it or not, Ezzie Phelan, you are one amazing person.
EZZIE:	Yeah, right! Look at me. Who'd want to be me? I'm pathetic!
RALDA:	Who's telling you that? You can't give in to that voice, Ezzie. You've got to fight it. *(sings)* There's another voice, a different voice, and you've got to find it. It's inside you, and it knows you so much better. There is no one in the world like you. Now you've got to let that voice come through. Ezzie Phelan, if you face life You will find that you embrace life. When you were born, the world made room She does for everyone The wonder is that each of us is totally unique I am who I am and you are you. You are you, a most expensive pearl A butterfly fresh out of its chrysalis
EZZIE:	*(sings)* You can't mean me.
RALDA:	In your heart there lies a golden key To secret beauty no one can dismiss
EZZIE:	So secret no one can find it
RALDA:	When you were born, the stars sang out
EZZIE:	They never sang for me
RALDA:	They do for everyone
EZZIE:	Well, then they must have been singing off-key
RALDA:	Some kind of inner knowing makes it all come down to this: I am who I am and you are you.
EZZIE:	*(speaking, not singing)* Is it really that simple?

RALDA: Yes.
(sings) We are all children of the dream
And love wraps us in its kindly beam
But all of us have times when life confounds us
We overlook our blessings

EZZIE: And the ordinary magic that surrounds us

BOTH: Surrounds us
You are you, a soul as true and fine
As rays of sunlight starting up the day
In your eyes, a flame that burns so bright
It cancels out a meteor's display
When you were born, the light burst through
It shines in everyone
No power in this universe can steal that light away
For I am who I am

EZZIE: You are who you are

BOTH: I am who I am and you are you.

End of song.

RALDA: I have to go now.

EZZIE: You can't go!

RALDA: I have to, Ezzie.

EZZIE: But what do I do now?

RALDA: Go out and take hold of life. It's yours, Ezzie. Don't let anyone take it away from you.

EZZIE: I want to. I want to in the worst way, now! But how do I hold on to this feeling?

RALDA: You'll find a way. Even when you lose it, you'll always find it again. I promise you. This time I mean it.

EZZIE: How can I go back there and face them?

RALDA: You can. You know that now.

EZZIE: But I can't do it alone!

RALDA: There are people in this world who love you just the way you are, Ezzie. If you really believe that, you'll find them. Goodbye, Ezzie.

EZZIE: Ralda, wait…

RALDA: Take good care of that emerald! *(she disappears)*

EZZIE: I can't do it without you!

EZZIE stands alone for a moment, taking in that Ralda is really gone. She holds up the emerald, looks at it, then looks over toward the playground, trying to summon up the courage to go back. She takes a deep breath and starts walking. A voice stops her.

VOICE: Just ignore them. Pretend you don't hear them.

EZZIE summons up her resolve and continues. Another voice makes her pause.

VOICE: If you could only lose a few pounds.

EZZIE tries to continue but still another voice intrudes.

VOICE: Everybody gets razzed — that's the way school is.

Followed quickly by another.

VOICE: Sorry, no geeks allowed.

EZZIE summons up all the resolve she can muster, but the voices start repeating and overlapping into a jumble.

VOICES: Just ignore them. Pretend you don't hear them. If you could only lose a few pounds. That's the way school is. No geeks allowed. Lose a few pounds. Ignore them. That's how it is. Just ignore them. Lose a few pounds.

EZZIE is paralyzed and can't move any closer to the playground. Gradually out of the jumble she begins to discern a singing voice: RALDA's.

RALDA: There's another voice, a different voice, and you've got to find it.

EZZIE: I don't have to listen to this stuff anymore!

As RALDA's voice grows louder, the jumble of other voices gradually recedes.

RALDA: It's inside you, and it knows you.

EZZIE: There are people out there who like me just the way I am.

RALDA: There's a light in you, no one can steal it.

EZZIE: I am going to take hold of my life, no matter what!

As EZZIE moves with determination toward the playground, her "inner" voices recede further and further, while the "hippo chorus" comes up again and grows louder and louder.

VOICES: Hippooo. Hippppooo.

JOSH returns. He and EZZIE arrive at the playground at the same time, but don't notice one another. They both look over in the direction of the voices and start shouting at the same moment.

JOSH: Hey, shut up, you guys!

EZZIE: Quiiiiieeeetttt!

The voices stop abruptly. EZZIE and JOSH notice one another's presence for the first time. They look at one another in astonishment and they start speaking at exactly the same time.

EZZIE: That was you!

JOSH: *(overlapping)* Was that you?

They try again, but still speak over one another.

EZZIE: Where'd you come…

JOSH: Thought you said…

They both laugh.

JOSH: You first.

EZZIE: You came back.

JOSH: Yeah.

EZZIE: Thanks.

JOSH: No problem. You look like you're feeling better.

EZZIE: I am. A whole lot better. And you know what?

JOSH: What?

EZZIE: If I lose this feeling…

EZZIE tosses the emerald at JOSH. He's startled but catches it and tosses it back to her.

EZZIE: I'll get it back!
               (sings) What do you know? I've got a voice inside I can rely on
               When things are tough, I know I'll get through it
               What do you know? There is a world out there I've got my eye on
               Now I'll find the place where I can belong
               Now that I know that I can stand my ground and be just who I am
               Nobody else is putting me down, 'cause I am strong
               Now I'm feeling whole
               And I can hear my soul singing a new song:
               I'm not somebody else, I'm me!

SHANNON and RALDA join EZZIE and JOSH.

EZZIE & CO: *(sing)* What do you know? There is a voice inside we can rely on (rely on)
When things are tough, I know I'll get through it (I believe that now)
What do you know? There is a world out there and we're a part of it
We found a place where we all belong (now I can belong)
Now that I know that I was wrong and I'm just fine the way I am
I feel the ground and I'm steady now (get ready now)
Heading on my way
I'm taking off today
I feel like I'm flying
Soaring into the sky
We fly, we fly, we fly.

*As the song ends, RALDA flashes her new pin: "Order of the Great Cosmic Emerald
Third Class."*

THE END

THE SEVEN RAVENS

A stage play in one act

Adapted from the Brothers Grimm
by Kathleen McDonnell

Jérome Sabourin, courtesy of Youtheatre

THE SEVEN RAVENS

I first came across this tale from the Brothers Grimm many years ago. I grew up in a household with six brothers and felt an immediate kinship with the heroine whose seven brothers are turned into ravens by their father's curse. I was moved by the bravery of this very young child who willingly goes to the end of the earth in search of her brothers, and was heartened to find a fairy tale in which a girl was the rescuer rather than the one being rescued.

I immediately thought of the story when Michel Lefebvre, the artistic director of Youtheatre in Montreal, asked if I was interested in adapting a Brothers Grimm tale into a play. To depict a whole range of characters — Little Dove, her parents and brothers, the Sun, the Moon and the Stars — with a cast of three, we drew on what is known as the "story theater" approach. In this style of theater the actors do it all: narration, manipulating puppets and playing multiple roles. The designers, Anne Barber and Brad Harley of Toronto's Shadowland Theatre, came up with the ingenious idea of having each of the seven brothers represented by a brightly-colored sweater on a clothesline.

For the second production the following season, Michel and I decided to try a different approach to the story, using two performers instead of three. This necessitated a major rewrite of the script, and the result was a much starker production distilled down to metaphorical essentials. This time the brothers were represented by seven black bird feathers, and Little Dove wandered in a shadowy forest of tall raven legs. The character of the Dwarf was renamed the Little Man, and he performed much of the narration as well as the voices of the brothers.

Both versions of *The Seven Ravens* are included in this book, as well as the original Brothers Grimm tale. If you read all three, you'll find they present an interesting contrast in how the same story can be adapted in different ways.

The Little Man (Clinton Walker) shows Little Dove's drawing of the seven ravens. From the 2002 production of The Seven Ravens.

The Seven Ravens
by the Brothers Grimm

There once was a man who had seven sons, but still he had no daughter, however much he wished for one. At length his wife again gave him hope of a child, and when it came into the world it was a girl. Their joy was great, but the child was sickly and small, and had to be speedily christened on account of its weakness. The father sent one of the boys in haste to the well to fetch water for the christening. The other six went with him, and as each of them wanted to be first to fill it, the jug fell into the well. There they stood and did not know what to do, and none of them dared to go home. When they still did not return, the father grew impatient, and said, "Those wicked boys must have forgotten what I sent them to do. They're probably playing games again!" He became afraid that the girl would die without having been baptized, and in his anger cried, "I wish those boys were all turned into ravens!" Hardly was the word spoken before he heard a whirring of wings over his head in the air. He looked up and saw seven coal-black ravens flying away.

The parents could not revoke the curse, and however sad they were at the loss of their seven sons, they still, to some extent, comforted themselves with their dear little daughter, who soon grew strong, and every day became more beautiful. For a long time she did not know that she had brothers, for her parents were careful not to mention them in front of her. But one day she accidentally heard some people saying of her, "the girl was certainly beautiful, but in reality she was to blame for the misfortune that had befallen her seven brothers." Then she was much troubled, and went to her father and mother and asked if it was true that she had had brothers, and what had become of them. The parents now dared to keep the secret no longer, but said that what had befallen her brothers was the will of Heaven, and that her birth had only been the innocent cause. But the girl took the matter deeply to heart, and decided that it was up to her to rescue her brothers. She had no rest or peace until she set out

secretly, and went forth into the wide world to seek her brothers and set them free, no matter what the cost. She took nothing with her but a little ring as a memento of her parents, a loaf of bread against hunger, a jug of water to quench her thirst, and a little stool to rest on when she became tired.

She set out, and went far, far away until she reached the end of the world. Then she came to the Sun, but it was too hot and terrible, and devoured little children. Hastily she ran away, and ran to the Moon, but it was far too cold, and also awful and malicious, and when it saw the child, it said, "I smell the smell of human flesh." She ran swiftly away, and came to the Stars, which were friendly and kind to her. Each one was sitting on its own little chair. But the Morning Star stood up and gave her the drumstick of a chicken, and said, "Without this drumstick you cannot enter the Glass Mountain, and in the Glass Mountain you will find your brothers." The girl took the drumstick, wrapped it carefully in a cloth, and walked and walked until she came to the Glass Mountain. The door was shut tight, and she thought she would take out the drumstick. But when she undid the cloth, it was empty. She had lost the gift of the kindly Stars.

What was she to do now? She was determined to rescue her brothers, and had no key to the Glass Mountain. So the brave sister took a knife, cut off one of her own little fingers, put it in the door, and succeeded in opening it. When she had gone inside, a little dwarf came to meet her, who said, "My child, what are you looking for?" "I am looking for my brothers, the seven ravens," she replied. The dwarf said, "My lords the ravens are not at home, but if you will wait here until they come, step in." Then the little dwarf carried the ravens' dinner in, on seven little plates, and in seven little cups, and the little sister ate a morsel from each plate, and from each little cup she took a sip, but in the last little cup she dropped the ring that she had brought with her. Suddenly she heard a whirring of wings and a rushing through the air, and then the little dwarf said, "Now my lords the ravens are flying home." Then they came, and wanted to eat and drink, and looked for their little plates and glasses. Then said one after the other, "Who has eaten something from my plate? Who has drunk out of my little cup? Here is the taste of human lips." And when the seventh came to the bottom of his cup, out rolled the ring. He looked at it, and saw that it was a ring belonging to his father and mother, and said, "Would to God our sister were here, then we would be free." When the girl, who was standing behind the door watching, heard that wish, she stepped forward, and on this all the ravens were restored to their human form again. And they embraced and kissed each other, and went joyfully home.

The End

Ben Philippi, courtesy of Youtheatre

THE SEVEN RAVENS

A stage play in one act
(2001 version)

Adapted from the Brothers Grimm
by Kathleen McDonnell

*The Star of Morning (Allana Harkin) gives Little Dove
(Nathalie Baroud) the key to the Glass Mountain.
From the 2001 production of* The Seven Ravens.

THE SEVEN RAVENS

This version of THE SEVEN RAVENS was first produced by Youtheatre, Montreal, Quebec in 2001 with the following cast and crew:

LITTLE DOVE	Nathalie Baroud
MOTHER	Allana Harkin
FATHER	Vincent Soars

Director:	Michel Lefebvre
Production Design:	Anne Barber and Brad Harley, Shadowland Theatre
Composer:	Allison Leyton-Brown
Lighting Design:	Mathieu Marcil
Stage Manager:	Luciana Burcheri

Cast of Characters:

DWARF
LITTLE DOVE (puppet)
MOTHER
FATHER
THE SEVEN BROTHERS / SEVEN RAVENS (puppets)
THE SUN
THE MOON
STARS/THE SEVEN SISTERS
THE STAR OF MORNING

All to be performed/manipulated by a cast of three

Prologue

The DWARF enters, making his way through the forest to the Glass Mountain.

DWARF   One for sorrow, two for joy
               Three for a girl, four for a boy
               Five for silver, six for gold
               Seven for a secret
               Never to be told!

The DWARF exits.

Scene 1

LITTLE DOVE theme music. A clothesline. Two smiling parents, FATHER and a hugely pregnant MOTHER enter.

MOTHER: Once upon a time lived a man and his wife.

FATHER: They had seven sons and a very happy life.

They carry a basket of clothes and begin to hang seven sweaters on the clothesline. He stops her as she bends down to get one out of the basket.

FATHER: Here, dearest, let me get it.

MOTHER: Oh, no, darling; I'm fine.

FATHER: No, no, I don't want you to go and strain yourself…

MOTHER: But I feel perfectly all right. After all, I've given birth to seven
               healthy babies already.

FATHER: And this one looks like it's getting ready to pop out any time now.

MOTHER: Yes, *(touching her swollen belly)* any time now…

FATHER: Just think…another baby…

MOTHER: Another child for our beautiful family…

FATHER: We're so lucky…

MOTHER: We're the luckiest people in the world…

FATHER: We have each other…

MOTHER: Each other…

FATHER: And our precious children…

MOTHER: Our seven dear, dear…

BOTH: Boys.

They turn toward the clothesline, now full of sweaters with names on them:
NED, FRED, TED, ED, RED, JED, ZED.
Under the parents' gaze, the clothesline suddenly erupts with a cacophony of voices
and antics.

BROTHERS: Who wants to play catch? Me! Me! Me too! No, you're too little. I
              am not!

FATHER: Boys, now stop fighting and try to get along.

BROTHERS: Mom, he kicked me. You started it. That's mine! I had it first.
              Give it back!

FATHER: I said no fighting. Your mother is going to have a baby any
              time now…

BROTHERS: Pop said stop fighting. Shut up! You shut up! I didn't do anything!
              It was him!

FATHER: …And she needs some peace and quiet!

BROTHERS: *(tapering off to a whisper)* Okay, pop. We're sorry! Mom needs
              peace and quiet. Peace and quiet. No talking! Shhhhh. Be quiet.
              Shhhhh…

FATHER: They can be such rascals…

MOTHER: They're pretty rambunctious…

MOTHER: You know what they say…

BOTH: Boys will be boys.

MOTHER: I love them all, but *(looking down at her belly)* I do hope it's a…

FATHER: Oh, me too! I hope it's a…

Parents look at one another. Their longing for a baby girl is palpable.
Suddenly MOTHER clutches her belly with a look of alarm.

FATHER: What is it?

MOTHER: I think it's time!

MOTHER groans with labor pains. FATHER comes to her assistance.
Panting, she pushes the BABY out. FATHER catches it. Parents look at one another
speechless for a moment, as if they can't believe their dreams have come true.

BOTH: It's a girl!

The BROTHERS, who have been silent through the birth, erupt again.

BROTHERS:　A girl! Hooray! Whoopee! It's a girl!

FATHER:　Look, boys. You have a little sister!

BROTHERS:　Yay! A sister! Whoopee! We have a sister! A little sister!! What's a sister? It's a girl, stupid! Hurray! We have a sister! Sister! Sister!!

FATHER returns BABY to MOTHER.

FATHER:　She's beautiful.

MOTHER:　She's everything we ever wanted.

Parents kiss, sharing a moment of pure contentment, which is broken by the BABY's cry. MOTHER tries to comfort her.

FATHER:　Is she all right?

MOTHER:　I'm sure she'll settle down. There, there, little one.

BABY continues to cry. MOTHER and FATHER look worriedly at her. Something's not right.

FATHER:　She doesn't look well…

MOTHER:　No, she doesn't. And she's so tiny…

FATHER:　Her color's not good…

MOTHER:　It looks like she's struggling for breath.

FATHER:　Oh, that's not a good sign…

MOTHER:　I think we should give her a remedy.

FATHER:　Yes! You're right. A remedy! I'll send one of the boys for it. *(to the biggest sweater)* Ed, go to the doctor down the street! Tell him your little sister is sick and needs a baby remedy right away.

BROTHER:　I'll get right on it, pop!

The other BROTHERS excitedly clamor to help out.

BROTHERS:　I wanna go get it! No me! I wanna to go. Can we all go, pop? Please, please?

FATHER:　Fine, you can all go. But come right back!

The SEVEN BROTHERS exit, babbling excitedly.

BROTHERS:　We will! We promise! We'll hurry! We'll be right back. Don't worry, pop!

MOTHER and FATHER worriedly hover over the cradle, rocking it.

MOTHER: Poor little thing.

FATHER: She'll be fine once she gets the remedy.

MOTHER: She's so pale...

FATHER: Those boys better not dawdle...

MOTHER: Her cry's getting weaker...

FATHER: ...Or start bickering with each other...

MOTHER: ...Like the life's draining right out of her...

FATHER: *(paces impatiently)* What's taking them so long? If they're fooling around in the village I swear I'll...

MOTHER: Look, she's gasping for breath!

FATHER rushes back over to look at the baby.

MOTHER: What if they don't make it back in time?

FATHER: Don't say such a thing!

MOTHER: We're losing her!

FATHER: No! No!

Hubbub offstage signals the BROTHERS' return. They enter, carrying a bottle of baby remedy.

BROTHERS: We're back, papa! We got it! We got the medicine!

MOTHER: Oh, thank heaven!

FATHER: Bring it here right away!

FATHER reaches out to get the bottle of medicine from them. They fight over it.

BROTHERS: Let me give it to him! No, me! I will! It's my turn! You carried it here! I asked first! I'm the oldest! I'm the littlest! I...

In their struggle the BROTHERS drop the bottle of medicine. It breaks with a crash on the floor. A moment of unbelieving silence all around. FATHER erupts in a rage.

FATHER: You idiots!

The BROTHERS cower in fear.

FATHER: Brats! You can't do anything right! Get out of my sight!

The BROTHERS flee his presence.

FATHER: Go on! The lot of you! Go turn into ravens!

As soon as the words are out of FATHER's mouth, all action stops, everyone freezes.

The music and soundscape signals the shift. Something terrible has been said that cannot be taken back, the equivalent of "go to hell!"

MOTHER and FATHER watch in horrified amazement as the BROTHERS are transformed into RAVENS. Once the transformation is complete, the RAVENS fly away with a great flapping of wings. Their exit is accompanied by a characteristic soundscape, which will recur later in the play.

FATHER: But I only meant to… I never thought… No… Come back… No!

FATHER exits, chasing after the RAVENS, then promptly returns.

FATHER: They're gone.

MOTHER: Gone?

FATHER: I tried to stop them, but they just flew off.

MOTHER: But what do we do? Will they come back?

FATHER: I don't know…

The BABY lets out a cry. They look down at her and are stunned by what they see.

MOTHER: Look!

FATHER: Her color is better.

MOTHER: Her breathing is stronger.

FATHER: She's getting better!

MOTHER: It's a miracle!

Parents fall into one another's arms, weeping with relief for a moment.
MOTHER tenderly lifts BABY out of the cradle and holds her.

MOTHER: We must take very good care of her.

FATHER: We'll never let anything bad happen to her.

MOTHER: She's all we have left now.

FATHER: She's our precious little dove.

They look at one another.

MOTHER: That's what we'll call her…

BOTH: Little Dove!

MOTHER hands the BABY, hereinafter called LITTLE DOVE, to FATHER, who tenderly cradles the BABY, then exits. MOTHER sadly goes and picks up the sweaters that dropped away when the BROTHERS were transformed into RAVENS. Melancholy lullaby and soundscape as she packs them away in a chest. She locks the chest and hides it away.

Scene 2

LITTLE DOVE, now a young girl, is alone, working feverishly on a drawing (the audience doesn't see the drawing just yet). Parents' voices are heard offstage.

MOTHER:	Little Dove?
LITTLE DOVE:	You can't come in yet!
FATHER:	Little Dove, what are you doing in there?
LITTLE DOVE:	I told you: it's a secret. I'm almost done.
MOTHER:	I'm sure you don't want your father and I to eat this delicious cake all by ourselves…
LITTLE DOVE:	I know you wouldn't do that, mama… There!

LITTLE DOVE rolls up her drawing into a scroll and hides it.

LITTLE DOVE:	Ready! You can come in now.

Parents enter, carrying a birthday cake with seven candles. They sing "Happy Birthday to You."

MOTHER:	Happy birthday, sweetheart!
FATHER:	Our precious little girl is seven years old today!
MOTHER:	Get ready to make a wish…

MOTHER holds out birthday cake. LITTLE DOVE, excited, is poised to blow out the seven candles. MOTHER and FATHER watch her, beaming with pride.

LITTLE DOVE:	I wish that my whole family would be as happy as we are right now, for ever and ever and ever!

She blows out all the candles in one go. Parents burst into applause, and hug her.

LITTLE DOVE:	Now we cut the cake!

MOTHER helps LITTLE DOVE guide the knife as she cuts three pieces.

LITTLE DOVE:	*(giving them each a piece)* Papa… Mama… and me!

They bite into their slices of cake.

ALL:	Mmmmm! Delicious!
LITTLE DOVE:	Oh, mama and papa, thank you for such a wonderful birthday. I love all my presents!
MOTHER:	And there's still one more gift.

LITTLE DOVE:	Really?
MOTHER:	Here, Little Dove. *(taking a ring off her finger)*
LITTLE DOVE:	But this is the one you always wear on your baby finger, mama. You can't give it to me! It's your prettiest ring!
MOTHER:	I want you to have it. My mother gave it to me on my seventh birthday, as her mother did before her. It's been in the family for many, many years, Little Dove. Now it's your turn to wear it.
LITTLE DOVE:	Thank you so much. I've never had a ring of my very own. It makes me feel so grown-up! And now… *(going to get the drawing she has rolled up and stashed away)* I have a present for both of you!
FATHER:	So that's what you've been doing in here!
MOTHER:	Little Dove, that's so sweet of you.

LITTLE DOVE proudly unrolls the drawing so parents and audience can see it. In her child-like hand, LITTLE DOVE has drawn a panoramic scene of beautiful, colorful birds. A stricken look comes over MOTHER's face.

LITTLE DOVE:	Don't you like my drawing, mama?
MOTHER:	Of course I do, dear.
LITTLE DOVE:	I thought you loved birds. That's why you named me after one!
FATHER:	That's right, Little Dove.
MOTHER:	It's a beautiful drawing.
FATHER:	We love it.
MOTHER:	I'm just tired, that's all. All the excitement of your birthday!
FATHER:	Yes, we're all tired. And it's way past your bedtime, Little Dove.
MOTHER:	Papa's right. It's late. Time for bed.
LITTLE DOVE:	Goodnight, mama.

LITTLE DOVE kisses MOTHER. FATHER and LITTLE DOVE exit.

MOTHER:	Goodnight, Little Dove. Happy birthday and sweet dreams.

Lullaby theme music as MOTHER is left alone on stage. FATHER re-enters. MOTHER holds her head in her hands, weeping silently. FATHER goes to comfort her.

MOTHER:	I miss them so much.
FATHER:	I know. But it's better to try not to think of them. It's too painful.

MOTHER:	I can't help it. Not a day goes by something doesn't remind me. And now Little Dove's picture… Don't you think it's time we said something to her?
FATHER:	No!
MOTHER:	But she has to find out sometime…
FATHER:	Why? What good would it do her?
MOTHER:	What if she finds out some other way? What if people in the village are talking and she overhears something?
FATHER:	Then we won't allow her in the village on her own!
MOTHER:	She's growing up! We can't be with her every second. It's time she learned the truth!
FATHER:	You must not say a word to her! I won't hear of it!
MOTHER:	I can't go on living like this! You want to pretend they never existed.
FATHER:	No, I simply want us to go on living our lives, for her sake. What else can we do? What's done is done.
MOTHER:	If only you'd never…
FATHER:	What?
MOTHER:	Nothing.
FATHER:	Go on, say it! If only I'd never what?
MOTHER:	If only you'd never opened your mouth maybe they'd still be…

During their argument LITTLE DOVE enters. They notice her in the doorway and abruptly stop talking.

LITTLE DOVE:	Mama…
MOTHER:	Little Dove! Why aren't you in bed?
LITTLE DOVE:	I couldn't get to sleep. Is something wrong?
FATHER:	No, Little Dove. Your mother and I are just talking. Now go back to bed.
LITTLE DOVE:	Will you tuck me in?

MOTHER goes over to LITTLE DOVE and notices, with a start, that she is dressed in one of her brothers' "name" sweaters.

MOTHER:	Little Dove, what have you got on? Where did you get this?

FATHER rushes over to see.

LITTLE DOVE:	I found a box of old clothes. Sweaters with all these funny names on them. I thought they were for dress-up…
FATHER:	I told you to get rid of them!
MOTHER:	I couldn't! They're all I have left!
LITTLE DOVE:	I'm sorry, papa. I didn't know, I was only playing…
FATHER:	I should have taken them all out and burned them years ago! Take that off, this minute!

FATHER pulls on one of the sleeves, tearing it off, shocking and frightening LITTLE DOVE; she has never seen her father so angry.

MOTHER:	Don't you see? We can't hide it anymore!
FATHER:	No!

LITTLE DOVE: Mama, papa! Please don't fight. I'm sorry I took the clothes out. I'll put them back and never take them out again. I promise!

MOTHER:	She must be told!
LITTLE DOVE:	Told what?
FATHER:	Don't say it!
MOTHER:	About your…
FATHER:	No!
MOTHER:	…Your brothers.

At the word "brothers," FATHER makes a gesture of agonized defeat.

LITTLE DOVE:	Brothers?
MOTHER:	Before you were born, we had other children, Little Dove. Seven boys.
LITTLE DOVE:	Seven? I have seven brothers?
MOTHER:	Yes, child.
LITTLE DOVE:	Where are they? Why haven't I ever seen them?
MOTHER:	Something happened to them. Shortly after you were born. A curse was put upon them.
LITTLE DOVE:	What kind of curse?
MOTHER:	One that turned them all into ravens!

LITTLE DOVE:	Ravens? Why?
MOTHER:	We don't know, Little Dove.
LITTLE DOVE:	When I was born? Were they turned into ravens because of me?
MOTHER:	No, Little Dove, it wasn't your fault. It was no one's fault. It was the will of heaven.
LITTLE DOVE:	What happened to the ravens? Where are they now?
MOTHER:	We don't know. They flew away. We looked and looked but we couldn't find them anywhere.
LITTLE DOVE:	I'll go look for them.
FATHER:	Listen to the child! I won't hear another word of this nonsense! Little Dove, I want you to forget everything you've heard tonight and never speak of it again!
LITTLE DOVE:	But papa…
FATHER:	You heard me! Now go on back to bed!

MOTHER silently indicates to LITTLE DOVE to obey. LITTLE DOVE exits.
MOTHER and FATHER exit. In her room, LITTLE DOVE can't sleep. She gets out of bed.
She quietly packs some things in a small bag or knapsack. She straps the pack over her
shoulder.

LITTLE DOVE:	I'll find my brothers and bring them home and then we'll all be together again. *(whispers)* Goodbye, mama and papa. Don't worry about me. I love you.

LITTLE DOVE exits. Lullaby theme is heard as she does.

Scene 3

The scene is transformed into The Great Wide World, a vast, open world — in contrast to
the enclosed home — where LITTLE DOVE will be on her own. A landscape.

LITTLE DOVE enters and makes her way through the world. The journey is accompanied by
a musical theme or soundscape that expresses the vastness of life, the smallness of the
girl, the difficulty of the task.

LITTLE DOVE:	I never knew the world was so big. How will I ever find my brothers in this Great Wide World?

LITTLE DOVE spies the SUN a short distance away.

LITTLE DOVE:	It's the Sun! Maybe she can help me.

> (sings)
> Have you seen my own dear brothers
> Flying near to heaven-o?
> Pray look kindly on my quest
> To find the ravens seven-o.

No reaction at first from the SUN. LITTLE DOVE approaches it.

LITTLE DOVE: Oh, Sun. You are so warm and I am so cold…

The SUN whispers ominously.

SUN: Come closer… closer…

LITTLE DOVE moves closer and closer.

LITTLE DOVE: I'm getting too hot…

SUN: … Closer… closer…

LITTLE DOVE: No!

LITTLE DOVE screams as she's nearly scorched by the SUN. She runs away.

LITTLE DOVE: Wow! That was close. I'll be more careful from now on. After all, I have a very important task: to find the Seven Ravens!

Lights go dim. Night is descending. LITTLE DOVE spies the MOON a short distance away.

LITTLE DOVE: The Moon! I hope he can help me.
(sings)
Have you seen my own dear brothers
Flying near to heaven-o?
Pray look kindly on my quest
To find the ravens seven-o.

The MOON is cool and remote. No response.

LITTLE DOVE: It's getting dark…

The MOON silently moves closer and closer to LITTLE DOVE.

MOON: (whispering) … Flesh…

LITTLE DOVE: Who spoke?

MOON: Flesh… I smell the smell of human flesh!

LITTLE DOVE recoils from the MOON in horror and runs away. She walks all the way to the End of the World.

LITTLE DOVE: I am so tired and hungry. But I ate all my bread and my water is all gone. What can I do? I don't know if I can keep going.

LITTLE DOVE:	*(sings)* I have searched the wide world over To the gates of heaven-o But none will help me in my quest To find the ravens seven-o.

LITTLE DOVE puts her head in her hands and cries. After a few moments, she lifts her head and looks around. There is the sound of music in the distance. It grows louder. Seven STARS appear. They do a happy dance, at the end of which they dissolve into giggles. They all talk at once, a girlish version of the SEVEN BROTHERS from the opening scene.

LITTLE DOVE:	Who are you?
SISTERS:	Can't you tell? *(more giggles)*
LITTLE DOVE:	You look like stars.
SISTERS:	That's exactly who we are! We are the stars known as the Seven Sisters!
LITTLE DOVE:	Oh, hello.
SISTERS:	Who are you?
LITTLE DOVE:	My name is Little Dove.
SISTERS:	Hello, Little Dove! We're very glad to meet you! Do you have any sisters?
LITTLE DOVE:	No.
SISTERS:	Oh, too bad.
LITTLE DOVE:	But I have brothers!
SISTERS:	Brothers? That's a silly word! What's a brother? We've never heard of brothers.
LITTLE DOVE:	Brothers are boys that are in your own family.
SISTERS:	Oooohhh…
LITTLE DOVE:	And I have seven of them!
SISTERS:	Ooohhh…
LITTLE DOVE:	But I can't find them anywhere!
SISTERS:	Too bad.
LITTLE DOVE:	I don't suppose you could help me find them?
SISTERS:	No. Sorry. We don't know any brothers.

LITTLE DOVE is upset, close to tears again.

LITTLE DOVE:	I don't know what to do! I've looked everywhere.
SISTERS:	Don't cry, Little Dove. We know someone who might be able to help you!
LITTLE DOVE:	You do? Who?
SISTERS:	The Star of Morning!
LITTLE DOVE:	Who's that?
SISTERS:	She's the one who comes out at the first light of dawn. She sees all kinds of things we can't see. I bet she's seen brothers.
LITTLE DOVE:	Where can I find her?
SISTERS:	She should be coming out right about… Now!

Fanfare as THE STAR OF MORNING (STAR OF MORN) enters, yawning.

SISTERS:	Hello, Star of Morning!
STAR OF MORN:	Good morning, my darlings! Did you have a good night?
SISTERS:	Oh, yes.
STAR OF MORN:	I'm glad. I had a wonderful sleep and now I'm ready to make everything look as beautiful as I am! And who is this little creature? One of my many fans, no doubt.
SISTERS:	This is our new friend. Her name is Little Dove.
STAR OF MORN:	Little Dove. What a charming name! You know who I am, of course.
LITTLE DOVE:	Oh, yes. You're the Star of Morning.
STAR OF MORN:	I am the dawn of the new day. No matter how dark the night has been, when I turn up everything looks bright and beautiful. That's why everyone loves me and they're so glad to see me.
LITTLE DOVE:	Oh.
STAR OF MORN:	At least, they're usually glad to see me.
LITTLE DOVE:	Oh, I'm very glad to see you! The Seven Sisters said you could help me.
STAR OF MORN:	Maybe. What kind of help do you need?
LITTLE DOVE:	I'm trying to find my brothers. They were all changed into ravens by a curse.

STAR OF MORN:	Oh, a curse.
LITTLE DOVE:	Have you seen any ravens?
STAR OF MORN:	Darling, I live in the sky. I see nothing but birds up here. Thousands and thousands of them.
LITTLE DOVE:	Oh.
STAR OF MORN:	But I might be able to help you find your brothers.
LITTLE DOVE:	Really? Do you know where they are?
STAR OF MORN:	No.
LITTLE DOVE:	But you just said…
STAR OF MORN:	I didn't say I knew where to find your brothers. But I do know where you can find some ravens…
LITTLE DOVE:	Ravens? Where?
STAR OF MORN:	Oh, I can't just tell you.
LITTLE DOVE:	Why not?
STAR OF MORN:	Because that's not how we do things here at the End of the World. We have to make it into a game.
LITTLE DOVE:	A game?
STAR OF MORN:	Yes, it's much more fun that way! The Seven Sisters will give you a riddle, and you have to solve it. Ready, girls?
SISTERS:	Below a base, atop a peak Inside's the very thing you seek.
STAR OF MORN:	Well? What is it?
LITTLE DOVE:	I don't know…
STAR OF MORN:	Need another hint? Girls?
SISTERS:	T'would be quite difficult to hide For anyone can see inside.

LITTLE DOVE thinks hard.

STAR OF MORN:	Come on, a base? A peak? See-through walls?
LITTLE DOVE:	I still don't know.
STAR OF MORN:	Oh, all right. You're new here. I'll give you this one. Girls?
SEVEN SISTERS:	The answer is the Glass Mountain!

LITTLE DOVE:	Glass Mountain? I've never heard of that…
STAR OF MORN:	Oh, you can't miss the Glass Mountain. I pass over it every day at the same time, and I always see these seven black birds flying around inside.
LITTLE DOVE:	Seven? That's got to be them!
STAR OF MORN:	Sometimes they bang right into the glass. Not too bright, those ravens!

LITTLE DOVE, excited, prepares to leave.

LITTLE DOVE:	Which way is it?
STAR OF MORN:	Hey! Not so fast!
LITTLE DOVE:	What?
STAR OF MORN:	Aren't you forgetting something?
LITTLE DOVE:	Oh! Thank you very much for your help.
STAR OF MORN:	No, no, no. How are you going to get inside the Glass Mountain?
LITTLE DOVE:	Oh. I didn't think about that…
STAR OF MORN:	Well, Little Dove, it's your lucky day, because I have the very thing you need.
LITTLE DOVE:	You do? *(pauses while she waits for STAR OF MORN to say something.)*
STAR OF MORN:	Oh, come now. You didn't think I was going to hand it to you on a silver platter, did you?
LITTLE DOVE:	Oh, right. The riddle. I forgot.
STAR OF MORN:	Ready, girls?
SISTERS:	What force and strength cannot get through This with a gentle touch can do.
STAR OF MORN:	Now, come on, that's an easy one…
LITTLE DOVE:	I'm trying… I just can't think of anything.
STAR OF MORN:	Fine! Girls?
SISTERS:	People at the door do stand Who do not have this thing at hand.
STAR OF MORN:	Give up?

LITTLE DOVE:	I don't know how to play this game!
STAR OF MORN:	A key, foolish girl! That's what you need to get into the Glass Mountain. A key!
LITTLE DOVE:	May I have it?
STAR OF MORN:	Of course not. You failed the test.
LITTLE DOVE:	Please, let me try one more!
STAR OF MORN:	Sorry, darling. You've used up all your tries.

LITTLE DOVE starts to walk away, dejected. She stops, turns around.

LITTLE DOVE:	It is cruel to pose a riddle to someone who is so… little!
SISTERS:	Ooohhhhhhh!
STAR OF MORN:	Oh, you're good. You're very good.
LITTLE DOVE:	Huh?
STAR OF MORN:	You've been stringing us along, you little devil!
LITTLE DOVE:	Oh no, I…
STAR OF MORN:	*(to SEVEN SISTERS)* Can you believe this one? Acting like she hasn't got a clue about riddles. Well, girls? What do you say?
SISTERS:	You played the game, but all this time You were cooking up a rhyme! And now it's plain for all to see Little Dove has won the key!

Brief reprise of the SEVEN SISTERS' happy dance as STAR OF MORN hands a stunned, jubilant LITTLE DOVE the "key."

STAR OF MORN:	Here it is.
LITTLE DOVE:	This is it?
STAR OF MORN:	Something wrong?
LITTLE DOVE:	No. It's just… It looks like a chicken bone.
STAR OF MORN:	It is a chicken bone. But it will get you into the Glass Mountain.
LITTLE DOVE:	Are you sure?
STAR OF MORN:	Of course I'm sure. But if you don't want it…
LITTLE DOVE:	Oh, no, I do! It's just…
STAR OF MORN:	What?

LITTLE DOVE:	Even if I do find the seven ravens, I still have to figure out how to change them back into my brothers.
STAR OF MORN:	And?
LITTLE DOVE:	I was wondering if you might know how to undo the curse.
STAR OF MORN:	Can the Star of Morning undo a curse? Is the grass green? Is the sky blue? Does a bear poop in the woods? I am the one who chases the dark away and makes everything bright and beautiful again! Remember?
LITTLE DOVE:	Oh, I'm so glad! But I know I have to guess another riddle, so go on, I'll do better this time…
STAR OF MORN:	(interrupting) Riddle? Oh, please. We are so done with that game.
LITTLE DOVE:	We are?
STAR OF MORN:	My dear, undoing a curse is serious business. If you want to find out how to bring your brothers back, you have to give me a gift.
LITTLE DOVE:	A gift? What kind of gift?
STAR OF MORN:	Something that will make me even more beautiful than I am now. Which is a tall order, I grant you.
LITTLE DOVE:	I don't have anything like… Oh, wait! I have this ring! My mother gave it to me for my birthday.
STAR OF MORN:	A ring? Oh, I can always use a nice piece of jewelry. Is it gold?
LITTLE DOVE:	No…
STAR OF MORN:	Does it have a precious stone?
LITTLE DOVE:	No…
STAR OF MORN:	Is it magic?
LITTLE DOVE:	I don't think so…
STAR OF MORN:	Darling, if it's not gold and it's not a precious stone and it's not magic then what possible interest would I have in some ordinary little ring?
LITTLE DOVE:	It's the only thing I have.
STAR OF MORN:	All this helping is making me tired and cranky. I really must go and catch up on my beauty sleep.
LITTLE DOVE:	But what about my brothers?

STAR OF MORN:	Oh, brothers, schmothers! Go home. Forgetaboutit!
LITTLE DOVE:	No, I've come all this way! I won't go home without my brothers!
STAR OF MORN:	Fine, whatever.

STAR OF MORN exits.

LITTLE DOVE:	*(calling after her)* The Seven Sisters said you were nice but you're not nice at all!
SEVEN SISTERS:	We're sorry, Little Dove. We tried to help.
LITTLE DOVE:	I know. It's not your fault. I don't care what she says. I'll find a way to undo the curse myself!
SEVEN SISTERS:	That's the spirit, Little Dove!
LITTLE DOVE:	I have to go now.
SEVEN SISTERS:	Wait, Little Dove! We have one more rhyme for you: All you have to keep in mind Is to look forward, not behind And when you don't know what to do Know that the answer lies with you!

The SISTERS dissolve into giggles one last time.

LITTLE DOVE:	Goodbye, Seven Sisters. And thanks!

LITTLE DOVE exits.

Scene 4

Melancholy lullaby theme comes up. Parents enter, looking bereft.

FATHER:	Why would she leave us?
MOTHER:	She said she wanted to go and look for them.
FATHER:	Was it because I got so angry? Oh, Little Dove. Did I drive you away, too?
MOTHER:	She's so young, out there all on her own…
FATHER:	I'm so sorry, Little Dove. Please forgive me.
MOTHER:	Come home to us, Little Dove. Wherever you are. Please come home!

FATHER and MOTHER embrace one another, weeping. They exit.

Scene 5

The DWARF enters, as at the opening of the play. The Glass Mountain and the RAVENS are seen in the distance. LITTLE DOVE enters. She approaches the Glass Mountain and peers inside.

LITTLE DOVE: Are they really there? I don't see any ravens. What if the Star of Morning was wrong?

She pauses a moment, stricken.

LITTLE DOVE: The chicken bone! Where'd it go? What'd I do with it?

She looks around frantically.

LITTLE DOVE: Did I have it in my hand? Did I put in in my pocket? I can't remember! I left in such a hurry…

She starts to run back the way she came.

LITTLE DOVE: It's so small. I could look and look and I'd never find it! What am I going to do? It's the only way to get into the Glass Mountain! How could I lose it?

LITTLE DOVE collapses in tears.

LITTLE DOVE: The Star of Morning was right. I'm just a stupid little girl. I hate myself!

The voices of the SEVEN SISTERS come back to her, from a far-off distance.

SISTERS: All you have to keep in mind
Is to look forward, not behind
And if you don't know what to do
Know that the answer lies with you.

LITTLE DOVE looks up.

LITTLE DOVE: Though I have lost the chicken bone…

She looks at her own hand.

LITTLE DOVE: I have one of my very own.

She makes her decision.

LITTLE DOVE: And for my seven brothers' sakes…

She raises her hand to the side of the mountain.

LITTLE DOVE: I will do anything it takes!

Closing her eyes to steel herself for the pain (like a child getting a needle) she slashes her baby finger on one of the jagged edges on the mountain's surface.

LITTLE DOVE: Owww!

She holds up the new "key," looks at her hand.

LITTLE DOVE: That wasn't so bad.

LITTLE DOVE puts the "key" into the lock and turns. It works. The door opens and she enters. Once inside, LITTLE DOVE spies the DWARF, who doesn't see her at first. She watches quietly a moment as he goes about setting a table with seven bowls, in which he places food.

DWARF: Who are you?

LITTLE DOVE: My name is Little Dove. I'm looking for the Seven Ravens. Have you seen them?

DWARF: Yes.

LITTLE DOVE: *(excited)* This really is the place? Where are they?

DWARF: My lords, the Ravens, are not at home.

LITTLE DOVE: When will they be back?

DWARF: What do you want with them?

LITTLE DOVE: They're my brothers.

DWARF: Your brothers? I don't think so.

LITTLE DOVE: It's true! They were changed into ravens by a curse. I'm going to take them home with me.

DWARF: This is their home now. They are better off here with me. See? I give them water in that bowl when they are thirsty. I feed them mice when they are hungry. They have forgotten their human life. Go back home and forget them.

LITTLE DOVE: No. I'm going to wait here until they come back.

DWARF: Suit yourself. I must go out and catch some fresh mice for their dinner.

LITTLE DOVE starts to move toward the table with the bowl of water.

DWARF: Stop!

LITTLE DOVE: I'm just getting a drink!

DWARF: Do not touch that! It is for my lords, the Ravens! I think I hear them coming now. You'd better hide. If they fly in and smell the smell of flesh, they might think you are a little rat and try to eat you.

RAVEN soundscape. DWARF exits. After he leaves, LITTLE DOVE moves toward the bowl of water. Hesitantly, she bends over to take a drink, her back to the doorway. The SEVEN RAVENS enter, hovering in the doorway. LITTLE DOVE hears the flapping of their wings and turns around.

LITTLE DOVE: It's you! I've finally found you! I've come so far, I've looked everywhere, I was afraid I'd never…

LITTLE DOVE stops, senses something is not right. A moment of tense silence. The RAVENS swoop down fiercely on LITTLE DOVE.

LITTLE DOVE: What are you…?

LITTLE DOVE shrinks away, trying to protect herself.

LITTLE DOVE: Please don't hurt me. I only came to…

LITTLE DOVE pulls free for a moment, but the RAVENS swoop down on her again.

LITTLE DOVE: No! Don't!

LITTLE DOVE waves her hands above her head, trying to fight them off.

LITTLE DOVE: Stop! Listen to me! I am Little Dove, your sister! I was born the day you turned into ravens.

The RAVENS continue to attack LITTLE DOVE.

LITTLE DOVE: You're human! It was a curse that changed you into ravens. Isn't there anything that will make you remember?

LITTLE DOVE suddenly has a thought, looks at her hand.

LITTLE DOVE: The ring! Look at this ring!

LITTLE DOVE takes the ring off her finger and holds it high for the RAVENS to see.

LITTLE DOVE: This is your mother's ring. She always wore it on her little finger. Remember? You saw it every day when you were growing up. When she held you and fed you and wiped your tears away. You have a mother! A human mother!

The RAVENS make croaking noises, as if trying to speak.

RAVENS: Maaawwww…

LITTLE DOVE: Yes, you do remember! I know you do! This ring belongs to your mother. Our mother.

RAVENS: Maaaaa… ther…

LITTLE DOVE: Yes! Keep trying to speak! That will undo the curse! I know it! Keep trying: Mother…

The RAVENS' efforts to speak grow more desperate and strained.

RAVENS: Maaa… ther… maaa… ther.

LITTLE DOVE: Yes! Mother!

RAVENS: Maaather…

LITTLE DOVE watches in shock as the RAVENS fall limply to the floor.

LITTLE DOVE: Oh, no. What have I done? I shouldn't have made you try so hard to speak. Please don't leave me. I don't care if you stay ravens forever. I want to be with you. You are my brothers. I love you.

As she says "I love you," LITTLE DOVE reaches out to gently touch the fallen RAVENS.

One by one, the BROTHERS pop out in a line. The seven sweaters re-appear, with names on them: NED, FRED, TED, ED, RED, JED, ZED. LITTLE DOVE is amazed and overjoyed.

BROTHERS: Look! We are back! We are back with our sister! Our sister, Little Dove! Look, I have arms again! Look, my old sweater! I love this sweater. We are back, Little Dove!

FATHER and MOTHER magically re-appear as well. They look at one another in a state of bewildered amazement, as if they can't quite believe what's happening to them. LITTLE DOVE rushes to embrace them.

LITTLE DOVE: Mama! Papa!

MOTHER: Little Dove!

FATHER: My little girl!

MOTHER: Thank God you're all right!

FATHER: We were afraid we'd never see you again, Little Dove!

LITTLE DOVE: Look, mama and papa! I did it! I found my brothers!

Parents look in utter stupefaction at animated BROTHERS.

FATHER: It's a miracle!

BROTHERS: Hey, mom and pop. Look! We're back! We're back!

MOTHER: Boys! My boys! Ned! Fred!

FATHER: Ed! Red! Jed! Zed!

BROTHER: Hey! What about me? I'm Ted!

MOTHER: Oh my precious Ted! We didn't forget you!

FATHER: Having you back is the most wonderful thing we could hope for! But how is it possible?

BROTHERS: It was Little Dove! She did it! Our sister, Little Dove! She brought us back. She's the best! Yeah! Hurray for our sister! Hurray for Little Dove!

FATHER: We don't know how you did it, Little Dove!

MOTHER: But you've done a very brave thing.

FATHER: You've made our family whole again. Thank you.

MOTHER: Now we can go home — together!

BROTHERS: Yeah! Home! Let's go home! I want to sleep in my old bed again! I can't wait to go home! Real food! Yeah! No more rats! Let's go home!

As they move to exit, LITTLE DOVE pauses a moment and talks to the audience.

LITTLE DOVE: Ravens, riddles, bones and rings
This world is full of wondrous things!
With help from friendly stars above
I searched and found the ones I love
But there is still much more to know
So through the Great Wide World I go!

LITTLE DOVE, the SEVEN BROTHERS and their parents dance through the Great Wide World, to jubilant musical accompaniment. LITTLE DOVE and her family continue on and disappear in the distance. The DWARF enters and speaks directly to the audience.

DWARF: First there were two,
Then came eight
Then seven flew
By the hand of fate
The little one's brought them back again
And two plus seven plus one make… ten.
Bo bow bended, this story's ended
If you don't like it, you may mend it!

THE END

Jérome Sabourin, courtesy of Youtheatre

THE SEVEN RAVENS

A stage play in one act
(2002 version)

Adapted from the Brothers Grimm
by Kathleen McDonnell

*The Little Man (Clinton Walker) beckons Little Dove
(Marjorie Chan) closer to the hot sun. From the 2002
production of* The Seven Ravens.

THE SEVEN RAVENS

This version of THE SEVEN RAVENS was first produced by Youtheatre, Montreal, Quebec in 2002 with the following cast and crew:

LITTLE DOVE	Marjorie Chan
LITTLE MAN	Clinton Walker
Director:	Michel Lefebvre
Production design:	Linda Brunelle
Sound design:	Nicolas Basque
Lighting design:	Caroline Ross
Stage manager:	Kieran Keller

This production of *The Seven Ravens* received a nomination for a Dora Mavor Moore Award for Outstanding Young Audience Production in 2003.

Cast of Characters:

LITTLE DOVE
LITTLE MAN
MOTHER
FATHER
BROTHERS (NED, FRED, TED, ED, RED, JED, ZED)
SUN
MOON
SEVEN SISTERS
STAR OF MORNING

Actors playing LITTLE MAN and LITTLE DOVE can double as PARENTS, BROTHERS, THE SUN, THE MOON, SEVEN SISTERS and THE STAR OF MORNING, as indicated.

Scene 1

As the AUDIENCE arrives, the LITTLE MAN greets and talks to them. When the play begins, LITTLE DOVE enters. The LITTLE MAN can see LITTLE DOVE but she is unaware of his presence. LITTLE DOVE stands poised to leave on a journey, holding a small loaf of bread and a water bottle, and wearing a small pouch. She looks resolute, determined.

LITTLE MAN: *(whispers)* Little Dove!

LITTLE DOVE hears something, looks around with a quizzical expression.

LITTLE MAN: *(whispers)* Don't forget to take your little stool.

LITTLE DOVE looks around again, pauses.

LITTLE DOVE: Oh, I almost forgot. I should take my little stool!

LITTLE DOVE gets the stool, tucks it under her arm and assumes once again the poised-to-leave stance. As the LITTLE MAN begins his story, however, LITTLE DOVE lies down and goes to sleep.

LITTLE MAN: *(to the AUDIENCE)* This is my friend, Little Dove. It might look to you like she's running away from home, but it's not what you think. She's not leaving her family, she's actually setting out on a mission to... Let me start at the beginning. Or rather, before the beginning...

Once upon a time lived a man and his wife.
They had seven sons and a very happy life.
Those seven boys were quite a handful...
The oldest was Ned. He was very mature and responsible...

NED: No problem, mom and pop. I'll get right on it.

LITTLE MAN: Next was Ted, an all-round athlete and fast runner, because he was always trying to keep up with his big brother...

TED: Hey, wait up!

LITTLE MAN: And then there was Fred, who was the clown of the family...

FRED: Hey, d'ja hear the one about the friar and the rabbi? Why'd the chicken cross the road? How many peasants does it take to light a candle...

LITTLE MAN: The next youngest was Red, who at times had quite a temper...

RED: Hey, somebody took my ball! Did you guys take my ball? Didn't you hear me say that nobody was supposed to touch my ball?!!

LITTLE MAN: Jed had a very sweet disposition, which was a good thing because he wasn't exactly the sharpest knife in the drawer…

JED: One and one are…? One and one are…? Rats, I knew the answer yesterday!

LITTLE MAN: And last but not least, the baby Zed, who, of course, was his mother's favorite…

OTHER BROTHERS: Zed is a mama's boy, Zed is a mama's boy, Zed is a mama's boy…

ED: Hey! What about me?

LITTLE MAN: Oh, wait, I almost forgot Ed. But that's what happens in a big family. Someone usually gets lost in the shuffle.

Each one of the boys had his own special place in his parents' hearts. But as much as they loved their seven sons, the man and his wife longed for a little daughter. One day, the wife went to her husband and told him some news: she was expecting a baby. They both looked forward to welcoming yet another child into their dear family. They embraced one another, and each said a silent prayer for God to bless them with a long-hoped-for baby girl. This quiet moment — as with most quiet moments in their household — ended quickly, as the boys came running into the house.

BROTHERS: Who wants to play catch? Me! Me! Me too! No, you're too little. I am not!

LITTLE MAN: "Now boys," their father said, "Stop fighting and try to get along."

BROTHERS: He kicked me. You started it. That's mine! I had it first. Give it back!

FATHER: I said no fighting. Your mother is going to have a new baby…

BROTHERS: Pop said stop fighting. Shut up! You shut up! I didn't do anything! It was him!

FATHER: She needs some peace and quiet!

BROTHERS: *(tapering off to a whisper)* Okay, pop. We're sorry! Mom needs peace and quiet. Peace and quiet. Shhhhhh. Be quiet. Shhhhhh. I didn't say anything…

LITTLE MAN: Time passed, until one day the wife began to feel pains in her belly. Her husband was about to tell one of the boys to run and get the midwife, but she knew there wasn't time; she'd had seven babies already, and each one had come more quickly than the one before. So she panted and pushed and panted and pushed and pushed and pushed and pushed and pushed… The father caught the baby as it emerged into the world. Immediately he looked to see whether… He handed the baby to his wife. They both looked at one another, speechless, as if they could hardly believe their prayers had, at long last, been answered… "It's a girl!" they both cried. "Look, boys. You have a sister! A new baby sister!"

BROTHERS: Yay! A sister! Whoopee! We have a sister! A little sister! What's a sister? It's a girl, stupid! Hurray! We have a sister! Sister! Sister!

LITTLE MAN: The father basked in his joy. But after a few moments he looked at his wife. She was holding the baby with a worried look on her face. "Something's wrong," she said. "She's not crying." For the wife knew that a baby always lets out a good, lusty cry right after it's born. Now they could both see that the baby was very tiny and sickly-looking. Her color wasn't good. She was struggling for breath. The man and his wife were very afraid. In those days many babies died soon after birth. Not only might they lose their precious daughter, but she might die without being christened. And without the baptismal waters to cleanse the stain of original sin, her soul would go straight to hell and burn forever in the fires of eternal damnation. They couldn't wait for the priest to come. They had to baptize the little girl themselves, right away. "Ned," said the man to his eldest son. "Take that jug to the well out back and get some baptismal water for your little sister. Right away!"

NED: I'll get right on it, pop!

LITTLE MAN: The other boys clamored to help out.

BROTHERS: I wanna get it! No me! I wanna do it. Can we all go, pop? Please, please?

LITTLE MAN: "Fine," said the man. "You can all go. But hurry!"

BROTHERS: We will! We promise! We'll hurry! We'll be right back. Don't worry, pop!

LITTLE MAN: The parents were beside themselves with worry. The baby was growing weaker and paler with every tiny gasp of breath. The boys raced to the well. Ted got there first and lowered the bucket. Red helped him pull it up, Ned held out the jug and together Red and Ted poured in the water right up to the brim. Ned stepped away from the well to rush back to the house with the jug, but Red and Ted pulled him back.

"Where are those boys?" the father cried. "What's taking them so long? If they're fooling around out there I swear I'll…"

TED:	Wait, I want to carry the jug!
RED:	No, me. I pulled the bucket up.
TED:	Too bad, I got here first!
LITTLE MAN:	Ned tried to stop the fight, saying, "I'm the oldest. Pop sent me to get the water." But Ted and Red kept pulling back and forth on the jug, then Fred and Jed and Ed, and even little Zed, jumped into the fray and they all started pulling on the jug…
BROTHERS:	Why not me? I wanna carry it. It's my turn. I never get to do anything!

The sound of a crash, pottery breaking, water spilling.

LITTLE MAN:	The jug fell to the ground and smashed into a thousand tiny pieces. The brothers froze. They looked at one another in terror, as the precious baptismal water seeped away into the earth. Their father knew exactly what had happened. He ran to the door, and shouted, "You brats! You can't do anything right! Curses on all of you! Go turn into ravens!" As soon as the words were out of his mouth, the man realized he had said a terrible thing. But it was too late. He heard a strange whirring noise in the sky overhead, and looked up to see seven coal-black ravens flying away. He tried to chase after them.
FATHER:	No! No, I didn't mean to… No, come back… Please, come back!
LITTLE MAN:	But the ravens flew over the pasture and disappeared into the woods beyond. The man ran back into the house to tell his wife what had happened. As he crossed the threshold he heard the baby let out a vigorous cry. "Come quick!" his wife called out. "Come see what's happened." He raced to her side and saw that the baby's color had changed dramatically. Her cheeks were a bright, healthy pink. Her little chest was rising and falling with each breath in a strong, steady rhythm. "She's going to be all right!" the wife cried. "It's a miracle!" The father gathered his wife and baby in his arms, and they wept tears of relief and gratitude. But then she asked about the boys, and he told her what had happened. At first she could not comprehend what he was saying… "Why didn't you bring them back?" she asked him. "I tried to," he replied. "They flew off into the woods beyond the pasture. There was nothing I could do. They're gone."

Gone!

The parents looked down at the baby and realized that now their little girl was all they had left in the world. They vowed they would take very good care of her, and never let anything bad happen to their precious little dove. At that moment their eyes met, and the very same thought arose in both their hearts. And so they decided right then and there to christen their daughter Little Dove. That night the only sounds in the house were the gentle back-and-forth of the rocking chair as the mother nursed her baby, and the strong, steady beat of Little Dove's heart.

As she grew older, they were careful never to speak about the sad and terrible circumstances of her birth. They kept to themselves, and never took her out into the village square, where she might overhear some of the neighbors talking about the mysterious disappearance of her seven brothers. They took care to remove all traces of the boys' lives from the house — their clothes and books and toys. It was as though their seven sons had never existed…

But unbeknownst to her husband, the wife had put aside a few of the boys' things and locked them away in a secret chest. Sometimes at night, when the other two were sound asleep, she would open the chest, take out a shirt or a ball and hold it next to her heart as she hummed a lullaby.

One for sorrow, two for joy
Three for a girl, four for a boy
Five for silver, six for gold
Seven for a secret
Never to be told.

Little Dove grew into a bright, beautiful little girl, full of life and high spirits. Of course, it didn't escape her notice that sometimes her father seemed distant and preoccupied, and that her mother at times seemed melancholy. But Little Dove thought that was just the way grown-ups were, and she made it her business to constantly look for ways to cheer them up — singing, telling jokes and playing games.

Finally it came around to Little Dove's seventh birthday. Her parents threw her a party with dancing and singing, and Little Dove was having such a wonderful time she didn't even think to ask why none of the other children in the village had been invited. As she blew out the candles on the cake, Little Dove closed her eyes and said: "I wish that my whole family would be as happy as we are right now, forever and ever and ever!"

Near the end of the party, her mother came to Little Dove and handed her a tiny box. Little Dove opened it eagerly. Inside was a small ring. "But this is your prettiest ring, mama. The one you always wear on your baby finger!" Her mother explained that on a child's seventh birthday, she always receives a special gift. The ring, she said, had been in her family for many, many years. Her mother had given it to her on her seventh birthday, and her mother before her. And now it was Little Dove's turn to wear the ring. "Thank you so much, mama," said Little Dove. "I've never had a ring of my very own. It makes me feel so grown-up! Oh, I almost forgot! I have something for both of you. A picture! I'll go get it."

The father and mother looked at one another and smiled. Little Dove was always drawing bright and colorful pictures, which they put on the walls all over the house.

"Turn around!" she called out to them. "And don't peek until I say you can. Okay, now!" As the man and his wife turned to look at Little Dove's picture, they were stunned by what they saw. In her child-like hand, Little Dove had drawn a large, panoramic scene of beautiful birds in a riot of color, some perched on branches, some soaring on the wind. A stricken look came over the mother's face. Despite herself, she let out a great, choking sob. Little Dove was mystified by her mother's reaction. "What's the matter, mama?" she asked. "Don't you like my drawing? I thought you loved birds. That's why you named me after one." Her mother quickly collected herself. "Of course I love your picture," she assured Little Dove. "It's a beautiful drawing," her father agreed. "But your mother is tired, with all the excitement of getting ready for your birthday. And it's past your bedtime, Little Dove."

Little Dove kissed both her parents and they bade her goodnight and sweet dreams. The man went to tuck her into bed. When he returned, his wife was weeping. He took her in his arms. "I miss them so much," she told him. "Not a day goes by that I don't think of them." "It's better to try and put them out of your mind," he replied. For that was his way of coping with his terrible grief. But now the wife looked up at her husband and spoke softly, choosing her words carefully. "Dearest," she said. "Don't you think it's time we told Little Dove the truth?" The man pulled away abruptly. "No!" he cried. "I won't hear of it!" His wife tried to reason with him. "She's growing up. We can't keep her shut up in this house forever. She'll be going out in the village on her own. Wouldn't it be better if she learned the truth from us rather than by accident from a neighbor?" But her husband was adamant. "No!" he said. "I forbid you to say anything to her."

Something in the man's tone of voice made his wife go rigid with anger. "How dare you forbid me to speak?" she said. "If you'd never opened your mouth none of this would have…." She held her tongue. But her husband knew exactly what was in her mind. "Go on, say it!" he cried. "If only I'd never said those words none of this would have happened. That's what you think, isn't it? After all these years, can you still not find it in your heart to forgive me?" There was a moment's silence. Then his wife turned away from him. "I don't want to talk about this any more," was all she said.

The man left the room and went to bed. His wife listened for the sound of his steady breathing. When she was certain he was fast asleep, she took out the secret chest. As she opened it she sang her plaintive lullaby…

One for sorrow, two for joy
Three for a girl, four for a boy
Five for silver, six for gold
Seven for a secret
Never to be…

"Mama?" The mother was startled at the sound of Little Dove's voice. "Little Dove! Why aren't you in bed?" "I couldn't get to sleep," said Little Dove.

The mother tried to quickly shove all the things back into the chest and put it out of Little Dove's sight, but the child hurried over to see what she was doing. "What are those, mama?" "Nothing," replied her mother. "Just some old clothes a neighbor gave me."

Fearful of waking her husband, the wife bade Little Dove to be quiet and ordered her back to bed, but Little Dove pleaded with her. "Let me look just a bit more, mama, please? There's toys in here, too. And the clothes are perfect for dress-up!"

With a catch in her throat, her mother watched as Little Dove rifled through the contents of the secret chest. The child would never know her brothers, but for these moments, at least, she could feel something of them. The wife was so caught up in her thoughts she didn't hear the footsteps coming from the bedroom. "What's going on here?" her husband called out. At the sound of his voice, the wife hurriedly stood up and tried to hide the chest. "Nothing, dear," she answered him. "Little Dove was having trouble getting to sleep." But before her mother could do anything to stop her, Little Dove ran over and held up some things from the chest to show her father. "Look, papa. Aren't these funny clothes?" The father was stunned at what he saw. "Where did you get those, Little Dove?" "From the chest…" she told him. "Chest? What chest??!"

The wife stood aside, realizing there was no point trying to hide it any longer. Her husband looked inside the chest and saw immediately that his wife had been deceiving him. "I told you to get rid of everything!" he thundered at her. "I couldn't!" she shouted back. "They're all I have left!" They began to argue fiercely. Little Dove was terrified. She had never seen her parents so much as raise their voices to one another. "Mama, papa! Please don't fight. I'm sorry! I'll put the things back in the chest. I'll never take them out again. I promise!!" But they kept on arguing, with the wife shouting, "I'm going to tell her!" and the man crying, "No, don't!" and Little Dove could make no sense of the volley of angry words, except for one which leapt out at her…

LITTLE DOVE suddenly sits up.

LITTLE MAN & LITTLE DOVE: Brothers?

LITTLE DOVE lies down, goes back to sleep.

LITTLE MAN: There was a terrible silence. The father turned away, a look of agonized defeat on his face. "There," he said coldly to his wife. "Now you've done it. I hope you're satisfied." Little Dove looked from one to the other. "Mama. Papa. What's going on?"

Her mother bent down and put an arm around Little Dove's shoulder. "Before you were born, Little Dove," she began, "We had other children. Seven boys." "Seven boys?" said Little Dove. "I have seven brothers? Where are they? Why haven't I seen them?"

Her mother explained that a curse was put on them shortly after her birth, one that turned them all into ravens. "A curse?" said Little Dove. "Why?" "We don't know," replied her mother. "It was the will of heaven. They flew off into the woods beyond the pasture, and we never saw them again."

The man couldn't bear to listen to any more. He told Little Dove to go back to bed, saying "I want you to put everything you've heard tonight out of your mind and never speak of it again." But Little Dove couldn't put it out of her mind. Even though she kissed her parents goodnight, as she always did, even though they bade her sweet dreams, as they did every night, she knew, as she lay down in her bed, that nothing was the same, and nothing would ever be the same again. Finally she drifted off into a restless sleep. In her dreams she saw ravens flying over the house and off into the woods beyond the pasture. And she heard her mother's voice singing the plaintive lullaby...

One for gladness
Two for mirth
Three for marriage
Four for birth
Five for sadness
Six for crying
Seven for an ache
That feels like dying...

Suddenly, Little Dove snaps awake.

LITTLE DOVE: Maybe it was my fault they were turned into ravens! My mother said it was the will of heaven. But what if it was because of me? I can't bear to see my mother and father so unhappy. I have to go find my brothers. I'll look and look and I won't stop until I find them and bring them home with me.

LITTLE MAN: She prepared to leave, taking with her a loaf of bread for when she got hungry and a jug of water to quench her thirst. On her baby finger, she placed the precious ring that her mother had given her for her seventh birthday.

LITTLE DOVE looks resolute, poised to leave, as at the beginning of the play.

LITTLE MAN: *(whispers)* Little Dove, don't forget your...

LITTLE DOVE: Oh! I almost forgot to take my little stool.

LITTLE MAN: Little Dove went to door of the cottage, paused a moment...

LITTLE DOVE: *(whispers)* Good-bye, mama and papa. I love you.

LITTLE MAN: ... And set off into the vast, dark stillness of the night. She began making her way across the pasture, but now, under the starlit sky, it seemed much bigger than in the daytime. She walked to the far end of the pasture, where a line of tall trees marked the edge of the forest. She turned back to take one last look at her home, and thought longingly of her warm, cozy bed and the delicious breakfast that would be waiting for her in the morning...

LITTLE DOVE: No. I will not turn back.

LITTLE MAN: She entered the forest. At first she could still see the light of the moon and the stars through the tops of the trees. But as she went deeper the forest grew thicker and thicker until she was completely enveloped in darkness.

LITTLE DOVE: I can't see a thing. I hope I'm going the right way.

LITTLE MAN: From time to time she thought she saw little eyes glowing through the darkness. And all around her were the night sounds of the creatures of the forest.

LITTLE DOVE: What was that? Oh, why did I do this? I'm too little to be out here all by myself. I just want to go home. But I can't tell which way to go. I'm just going to sit here and wait until it's daylight. Then I'll be able to see my way home.
(sings) One for sorrow, two for joy, three for…
No, I don't want to sing that one.

LITTLE DOVE grows more and more sleepy, until she finally nods off.

LITTLE MAN: Little Dove fell fast asleep. When she woke up, sunlight was streaming through the treetops.

LITTLE DOVE: I feel a lot better now. I don't want to go back home. I'm going to keep going and find my brothers.

LITTLE MAN: Now, in the daylight she was able to find her way through the forest. She walked and walked for what felt like a very long time. When she finally emerged from the tall trees, she was amazed to discover that beyond the forest next to the pasture by her home — the forest that she had looked upon every day of her young life — lay a Great Wide World.

LITTLE DOVE: I never knew the world was so big!

LITTLE MAN: Little Dove forgot all about her fears. Eager to explore this place she had never known existed, she went skipping off into the Great Wide World. Back at the cottage, the man and his wife woke up in the morning and found Little Dove gone. They were devastated. Their anger at one another was swept aside, as they vowed to go to the ends of the earth to find Little Dove. They set off through the pasture to the edge of the forest, calling, "Little Dove! Where are you? Little Dove! Little Dove!" Meanwhile, Little Dove was still making her way through the Great Wide World.

LITTLE DOVE: *(exhausted)* I never knew the world was so big. And I haven't seen any ravens anywhere!

LITTLE MAN: She walked and walked and walked and walked, until finally she came to the end of the world. She sat down on her little stool to rest a while. Out of the corner of her eye she saw a bright light, and felt a warmth surrounding her. She looked up and saw the Sun, so low in the sky she could almost reach out and touch it.

LITTLE DOVE: Oh, Sun, you see everything in the sky. Can you help me?
(sings) Have you seen my own dear brothers
Flying near to heaven-o?
Pray look kindly on my quest
To find the ravens seven-o.

LITTLE MAN: The Sun nodded and said, "Come closer, closer." And indeed the Sun's rays felt warm and comforting to Little Dove, and its bright light began to restore her spirits.

LITTLE DOVE: Oh, Sun. You feel so good on my skin…

LITTLE MAN: But as she moved still closer the Sun's warmth didn't feel good anymore.

LITTLE DOVE: I'm getting so hot. Almost like I've got a fever.

LITTLE MAN: And still the Sun urged her on: "Come closer… closer… closer…"

LITTLE DOVE: No! You don't want to help me. You want to burn me up until I'm nothing at all! I'm getting as far away from you as I can.

LITTLE MAN: Little Dove backed away from the scorching Sun. She watched with great relief as it dropped lower and lower in the sky.

LITTLE DOVE: I must be more careful from now on. Just because someone looks nice doesn't mean they are.

LITTLE MAN: As the cool of the evening came on, she spied the Moon peeking out over the edge of the horizon.

LITTLE DOVE: Hello, Moon! I bet you can help me. You see just as much of the sky as the Sun.
(sings) Have you seen my own dear brothers
Flying near to heaven-o?
Pray look kindly on my quest
To find the ravens seven-o.

LITTLE MAN: The Moon made no reply but simply smiled and nodded at her to come a little closer.

LITTLE DOVE: Well, I don't know if I should. But… you won't burn me up like that nasty old Sun. Okay!

LITTLE MAN:	As she approached the Moon she heard a voice whispering, "Flesh… Flesh…"
LITTLE DOVE:	Who's that?
LITTLE MAN:	"I smell the smell of human flesh…" Little Dove began to feel a chill right down to the marrow of her bones. Her teeth began to chatter, and her skin grew numb. As she looked up, she could see that the Moon's smile had become a monstrous, devouring mouth.
LITTLE DOVE:	No! Leave me alone! I see who you really are. You want to freeze my body hard as ice and gnaw away at my flesh until I am nothing at all!
LITTLE MAN:	Little Dove ran away from the cold, ravenous Moon. She ran and ran until she couldn't run any more. Now she was hungry, but she had eaten up her little loaf of bread, and her water jug was empty. Exhausted and discouraged, she sat down on her little stool to rest.
LITTLE DOVE:	*(sings)* I have searched the wide world over To the gates of heaven-o But none will help me in my quest To find the ravens seven-o.
LITTLE MAN:	She felt so tired, it was all she could do to keep from lying down and drifting off to sleep. She thought she heard the sound of voices in the distance. Perhaps it was a dream. Or perhaps she had died and it was the angels come to take her up to heaven. As the sound of the voices continued she realized that it was the sound of… laughter.
LITTLE DOVE:	Who's there?
LITTLE MAN:	Little Dove lifted her head and looked up at the sky. Seven Stars glittered above her in the heavens, each one sitting on its own little stool. They were tossing a ball back and forth among them with a constant stream of giggles. The ball was so light and airy it seemed to be made of nothing but cloud, and sometimes it started to float away from them, which made the Stars laugh even harder as they leapt off their stools straining to catch it. Little Dove watched them in delight and amazement, and for a moment, she completely forgot her own trials.
LITTLE DOVE:	Can I play with you?

LITTLE MAN:	The Stars looked down at her. "Who're you?"
LITTLE DOVE:	My name is Little Dove. See, I have a stool too!
LITTLE MAN:	The Stars were impressed at the sight of Little Dove's stool. "Oohhhhh!" they cried. "Here, Little Dove. Catch!" Suddenly the light and airy ball came sailing toward Little Dove. She stretched her arms high over her head, caught the ball and immediately tossed it back up toward the Stars.
LITTLE DOVE:	I never knew Stars could play ball.
LITTLE MAN:	"We're not just any old stars," they informed her. "We are the Seven Sisters!"
LITTLE DOVE:	Seven Sisters? Really? You're all sisters?
LITTLE MAN:	The Seven Sisters thought this was a terribly silly question. They broke into peals of laughter. "Of course we are," they said. "Aren't you?"
LITTLE DOVE:	Aren't I what? Oh, I see what you mean. Yes, I am a sister. But I don't have sisters like you.
LITTLE MAN:	The Seven Sisters were perplexed by Little Dove's words. "Is this a riddle?" they asked her. "How can you be a sister if you don't have any sisters?"
LITTLE DOVE:	It's not a riddle, you sillies! I have brothers. I am the sister of my brothers.
LITTLE MAN:	This was a concept that was completely outside the Seven Sisters experience. "Brothers?" they exclaimed. "What is a brother? We have never heard of brothers."
LITTLE DOVE:	Brothers are boys that are in your own family. And I have seven of them!
LITTLE MAN:	Now the Seven Sisters were really impressed. "Seven brothers? Ooohhh…"
LITTLE DOVE:	But they went away when I was born. I've walked all the way to the end of the world looking for them. I've looked and looked and I can't find them anywhere. I don't suppose you could help me find them?
LITTLE MAN:	Little Dove looked eagerly at the Seven Sisters, but all they could do was shake their heads. "Sorry, Little Dove. We don't know any brothers."

LITTLE DOVE:	Oh.
LITTLE MAN:	"But we know someone who might be able to help you."
LITTLE DOVE:	You do? Who?
LITTLE MAN:	"The Star of Morning!"
LITTLE DOVE:	The Star of Morning? Who's that?
LITTLE MAN:	The Seven Sisters all talked excitedly at once. "She's a wishing star! She comes out at the first light of dawn! She can help you see things in a different light. She makes the whole world look bright and beautiful."
LITTLE DOVE:	Maybe she can help me find my brothers! Where can I find her?
LITTLE MAN:	"Just wait a little while. She'll be coming out soon."
	Little Dove reached up again as the light and airy ball came sailing her way. But just as she was about to catch it, the ball suddenly disappeared. The laughter of the Seven Sisters came to an abrupt halt.
LITTLE DOVE:	What's going on?
LITTLE MAN:	"The game's over. We have to go."
LITTLE DOVE:	Go? What do you mean? Where are you going?
LITTLE MAN:	"It's almost the dawn of the new day, Little Dove. We are the Seven Sisters. We only shine at night."
LITTLE DOVE:	No, wait… Come back!
LITTLE MAN:	"Good-bye, Little Dove."
	The seven twinkling Stars disappeared as their voices faded away in the pre-dawn sky. Little Dove had had such fun with the Seven Sisters. But now she was all alone again. There was nothing to do but sit on her little stool and wait for the Star of Morning to appear. She sat for what seemed like a very long time. Even though she knew that the dawn was imminent, the sky above her seemed darker then ever. She felt a loneliness deeper than anything she had ever felt before. Would the morning ever come?
LITTLE DOVE:	Will I ever find my brothers?
LITTLE MAN:	Or was she doomed to wander the Great Wide World forever? At long last, she thought she spied a tiny pinpoint of light off in the distance.

LITTLE DOVE:	Is that her? Is that the Star of Morning?
LITTLE MAN:	The point of light grew steadily larger and larger. Finally she could see that it was a great, glowing hand coming toward her out of the darkness. She wondered: could this really be the help she had been awaiting for so long?
LITTLE DOVE:	Are… you the Star of Morning?
LITTLE MAN:	In answer, a voice came out of the darkness.
STAR OF MORN:	Do not seek your own dear brothers Flying near to heaven-o Within the mountain made of glass You'll find the ravens seven-o.
LITTLE DOVE:	The mountain made of glass? Where is that?
LITTLE MAN:	The voice made no reply. But the great, glowing hand pointed far off into the distance. When Little Dove looked in that direction she could see what looked like the glistening peak of a mountain.
LITTLE DOVE:	Yes, that looks like it could be it!
LITTLE MAN:	She was about to race off in the direction of the Glass Mountain, but then a thought occurred to her.
LITTLE DOVE:	Wait. You said I'd find my brothers inside the Glass Mountain. How am I supposed to get inside a mountain? I'm not going to let myself be fooled again. How do I know you're telling the truth? You have to give me some sign.
LITTLE MAN:	Now the glowing hand loomed right over Little Dove's head, almost as if poised to strike her. For a moment she recoiled in fear. But then she noticed that there was something lying in the palm of the great hand. It seemed to her that the hand was holding the object out to her, as if urging her to take it.
LITTLE DOVE:	What's that? It looks like a chicken bone.
LITTLE MAN:	Now the voice of the great hand spoke up.
STAR OF MORN:	What force and strength cannot get through This with a gentle touch can do.
LITTLE DOVE:	What? Is that some kind of riddle? I don't have time for riddles right now. I have to go find my brothers!
LITTLE MAN:	But the voice spoke again.

STAR OF MORN: If you wish to step inside
Turn and it shall open wide.

LITTLE DOVE: Turn? Is that some kind of key? That must be it! The Glass Mountain has a door and this chicken bone is the key to it! Am I right?

LITTLE MAN: The voice remained silent. Finally Little Dove reached out and took the chicken bone from the great hand of the Star of Morning.

LITTLE DOVE: The Seven Sisters were right. They said you'd help me. Thank you, Star of Morning. Thank you so much!

LITTLE MAN: Little Dove prepared to run off in the direction of the Glass Mountain, but the voice of the Star of Morning came forth one more time.

STAR OF MORN: When you upon the threshold stand
Enter there by your own hand.

LITTLE DOVE: What? Oh, I will. Goodbye, Star of Morning. Thanks again!

LITTLE MAN: Quickly she set off in the direction of the Glass Mountain. In the distance it looked like an enormous crystal gleaming in the sun. She ran as fast as she could, until the Glass Mountain loomed over her like a great wall of ice. She walked round and round the magnificent crystal, looking in amazement at its gleaming surface, dappled with beautiful rainbows by the Sun's rays. But she was careful to avoid the sharp points and jagged shards of glass that thrust out here and there. Finally she found a door with a keyhole etched right into the glassy surface.

LITTLE DOVE: Here it is!

LITTLE MAN: She reached into her pouch for the chicken bone. But she couldn't find it. She rooted around everywhere inside the pouch.

LITTLE DOVE: Where'd it go? What'd I do with it? I thought it was in my pouch. Did it fall out?

LITTLE MAN: It was gone. Little Dove had lost the chicken bone, the gift of the Star of Morning. Frantically, she began to retrace her steps. But she'd walked so far around the Glass Mountain and been so taken with its beauty that she hadn't been paying attention, and she had no idea which direction she'd come from. There was no use looking for the chicken bone. It was too small. She could look and look and never find it.

LITTLE DOVE: Now what am I going to do? I'm so close. I've ruined everything. What was I thinking? I can't rescue my brothers. I can't do anything. I'm just a stupid little girl.

LITTLE MAN: Little Dove fell to her knees and wept the bitterest tears she'd ever wept in her young life. She had come so far, had withstood so many trials and dangers, but it was all for nothing. The time had come for her to give up and go home.

LITTLE DOVE: I'd rather die than go back to my parents with nothing!

LITTLE MAN: *(whispers)* It's no use, Little Dove. Go home.

LITTLE DOVE: There's got to be some other way to get into the Glass Mountain.

LITTLE MAN: *(whispers)* There isn't, Little Dove. It's all over. Give up.

LITTLE DOVE: No! I am not going to give up! I'm going to find a way to get inside! The Star of Morning didn't say the chicken bone was the only way, she said… What was the last thing she said?

"When you upon the threshold stand, enter there by your own hand"… By your own hand… By my own hand… By my own baby finger, where I wear the ring my mother gave me…

I do not need a chicken bone
I have a key here of my own
Now for my seven brothers' sakes
I will do anything it takes!

I walked over to the Glass Mountain and looked for the sharpest, most jagged edge I could find. Taking a deep breath to steel myself against the pain, I raised my hand and slashed my baby finger against the glass… Owwwww! I carried it to the door of the Glass Mountain and inserted the tiny protruding bone into the keyhole. I turned it, and the door flew open.

I stepped inside the Glass Mountain. It was like a vast cathedral with a ceiling of blue sky. I was so overwhelmed by its grandeur that I nearly jumped out of my skin when I heard a noise behind me. I turned around to see what it was. Before me stood a strange little man, holding a water jug. He was standing at a long table, on which were set seven little bowls and seven little cups. He set down the water jug and turned to me.

LITTLE MAN:	Who are you?
LITTLE DOVE:	My name is Little Dove. I'm looking for the Seven Ravens. Have you seen them?
LITTLE MAN:	Yes.
LITTLE DOVE:	This really is the place? Where are they?
LITTLE MAN:	My lords, the Ravens, are not at home.
LITTLE DOVE:	When will they be back?
LITTLE MAN:	What do you want with them?
LITTLE DOVE:	They're my brothers.
LITTLE MAN:	Your brothers?
LITTLE DOVE:	Yes! They were changed into ravens by a curse. I'm going to take them home with me.
LITTLE MAN:	I'm afraid that is not possible.
LITTLE DOVE:	What do you mean?
LITTLE MAN:	This is their home now. They are better off here with me. I give them water in those bowls when they are thirsty. I feed them mice when they are hungry.
LITTLE DOVE:	But when they see me, I know they'll want to come home…
LITTLE MAN:	My lords, the Ravens, have forgotten their human life. It will be much better for them, and for you, if you go back home and forget them.
LITTLE DOVE:	I can't do that! I've come all this way…
LITTLE MAN:	I am sorry you've wasted your time.
LITTLE DOVE:	Let me just wait until they come back!
LITTLE MAN:	If you do, you will be in great danger.
LITTLE DOVE:	Why?
LITTLE MAN:	When they come in and smell the smell of flesh, they will think you are a little rat and try to eat you.
LITTLE DOVE:	I don't care. I'm going to stay right here.
LITTLE MAN:	Fine. Suit yourself. You will see that nothing you do will make any difference. I must go out and catch some more fresh mice. Do not

touch anything on the table while I am gone. That is for my lords, the Ravens.

LITTLE MAN exits.

LITTLE DOVE: I knew better than to trust the little man. I figured he'd gone outside to wait for the Ravens so he could poison their minds against me. Quickly, I took a taste from each of the little bowls, and drank from each of the little cups. I took the ring from my baby finger and dropped it in the last cup. Then I scrambled under the table to hide. I waited until I heard a great whirring of wings. The door of the Glass Mountain opened. The little man entered and behind him hovered the Seven Ravens. I was so excited to see them I almost leapt right out from under the table, but wisely, I held back, waiting for just the right moment. The little man looked around and shrugged, believing that he had succeeded in scaring me away. Then he bowed toward the Ravens.

LITTLE MAN: Your dinner is ready, my lords.

LITTLE DOVE: The Ravens flew over to the table and each began to eat from his own little bowl, and drink from his own little cup, all but one, who spoke up, saying, "I smell human flesh." The little man shook his head, saying…

LITTLE MAN: No, my lord. It is only the smell of the delicious rat waiting in your bowl.

LITTLE DOVE: But then another Raven looked up and said, "Who has been eating from my little bowl? I taste the taste of human lips." The little man shook his head more insistently and said…

LITTLE MAN: No, my lord. A pesky little animal came in and nipped at your bowl, but I chased it away.

LITTLE DOVE: Then the smallest of the Ravens looked up and said, "What is this in the bottom of my little cup? It looks like a ring from a human finger." At that the little man sprang up and shouted angrily…

LITTLE MAN: Ring? What ring?

LITTLE DOVE: But it was too late. The little man let out a great, agonizing groan of defeat…

LITTLE MAN: Noooo!

LITTLE DOVE: … As I boldly stepped out from under the table and showed myself to the Ravens.

That is your mother's ring. She wore it on her little finger. You saw it every day when you were growing up. When she held you and fed you and wiped your tears away. You have a human mother and a human father and a human sister. My name is Little Dove. I am your sister.

The Ravens grew excited and began speaking all at once, in great croaking voices… "Sister… Sister…" But their efforts to speak grew more desperate and strained. "Sister… Sister…" Till finally I watched in horror as the Ravens dropped their wings and fell limply to the floor, their featherskins lying in heaps like crumpled shirts.

LITTLE MAN: Now look what you've done! You have murdered my lords, the Ravens!

LITTLE DOVE: I knelt down beside the pile of featherskins.

No. Please don't leave me. I don't care about the curse. I don't care if you stay ravens forever. You are my brothers. I love you.

I gently stroked and caressed the fallen Ravens. Then, an astounding thing happened: the featherskins began to rustle and stir. And one by one by one, seven human figures emerged out of the pile: Ned, Fred, Ted, Red, Jed and little Zed!

ED: Hey! What about me? I'm Ed!

LITTLE DOVE: Oh, Ed, I wouldn't forget you!

BROTHERS: Look! We are back! We are back with our sister! Our sister, Little Dove!

LITTLE DOVE: I was so afraid I'd never find you! Now we can all go home together. Our parents will be so happy to see you again!

BROTHERS: Yeah, let's go home and see mom and pop! We'll sleep in real beds. Eat real food. No more slimy rats! Hurray for our sister! Hurray for Little Dove!

LITTLE DOVE: As my brothers set out on their journey home, I paused a moment in the doorway of the Glass Mountain. I watched the little man as he gathered up the seven little bowls, put away the seven little cups, and swept away the pile of lifeless featherskins. All these seven years he had lived with the Ravens, but now that they were human, they knew him not. "Good-bye," I said. "Thank you for taking such good care of my brothers." Then I stepped outside the

Glass Mountain and ran to catch up with my brothers as together we danced off into the Great Wide World.

LITTLE MAN: One for sorrow
Two for joy
Three for a girl
Four for a boy
Five for silver
Six for gold
Seven for a secret
Now is told

LITTLE MAN: Bo bow bended, this story's ended

LITTLE DOVE: If you don't like it, you may mend it!

THE END

FOUNDLINGS

A play in two acts

Written by Kathleen McDonnell

Ron Chambers, courtesy of the University of Lethbridge

FOUNDLINGS

The seed of *Foundlings* was planted when I came across a historical book about "foundlings," infants abandoned by their families, who were then found and raised by others. Over the next few years, a story took shape in my mind. It was set in ancient Greece, which allowed me to draw on the rich mythology and history of the period. Our notions about the ancient Greeks tend toward images of people in togas walking through pristine white-columned temples, spouting philosophical ideas. I wanted to depict a more rough-and-ready world, populated by characters who look, talk and act more like people today, who grapple with the same problems we do.

The play is set in the fifth century B.C., during a period of great upheaval, with the rise of democracy, the transition from barter to a money-based economy, and changing ideas about the gods and their role in human destiny.

The story is a mixture of history and fiction. For example, female babies in ancient Greece were known to have been abandoned more often than males, but the story about Alecto (a girl) being nursed and raised by a bear is my own invention. I borrowed elements of the story from a number of well-known myths and other tales. The characters of Baucis and Philemon appear in a story (told in Ovid's Metamorphoses, and retold as "The Miraculous Pitcher" in Nathaniel Hawthorn's *A Wonder Book*) about an elderly couple who are visited

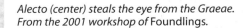

Alecto (center) steals the eye from the Graeae.
From the 2001 workshop of Foundlings.

by the god Hermes and rewarded for their kindness to a stranger. The Graeae are one-eyed hags borrowed from the tales of Perseus' exploits. Alecto's story is reminiscent of a number of abandonment stories in the ancient world, the best-known being the foundling twins, Romulus and Remus, who went on to establish the city of Rome.

Foundlings is the only two-act play in this book. It has a larger cast and was written to be performed in a theater rather than as a touring show. It is also aimed at an older age group — 12 and up — than the other plays in this book. In 2001, the play received a month-long workshop directed by Annie Szamosi, with the participation of students in the theater department at the University of Lethbridge in Alberta. In a workshop, the director and cast work with the playwright to improve the script, and try out different ways of performing it. In the *Foundlings* workshop we explored a variety of techniques, including masks, choral singing and stilt-dancing, and I re-wrote a good deal of the play based on what I learned in the workshop sessions.

FOUNDLINGS

The play is set in Greece in the mid-fifth century B.C., and the action takes place in and around the agora, or public square, of Argenopolis, a fictional polis or city-state.

Cast of Characters:

Gods:

      ARTEMIS, the huntress, daughter of Zeus
      ZEUS, king of the gods of Olympus
      ATHENE, patroness of Athens, also daughter of Zeus
      HERMES, the messenger, son of Zeus
      ION, a half-god, half-mortal youth, and grandson of Zeus
      The GRAEAE ("gray ones"), ancient hag-goddesses
      A NYMPH

Mortals:

      CLEON, leader of the Assembly of Argenopolis
      DIAGORAS, age 17, a champion athlete
      PHILEMON, a teacher/Sophist, father of Diagoras
      BAUCIS, a potter, mother of Diagoras
      ALECTO, age 17, an abandoned "wild child"
      ZOE, age 12-13, a household slave
      THYESTES, a student
      A WOMAN
      A FOREMAN (offstage voice)
      A SHE-BEAR

Casting note:

If players take on multiple roles, *Foundlings* can be performed with a cast of eight: five males, three females (5M, 3F).

Hermes and Ion masquerade as an Oracle and her priestess.
From the 2001 workshop of Foundlings.

ACT I
Scene 1: Prologue

The outskirts of Argenopolis, just before dawn. ARTEMIS is practicing with her bow and arrow. She hears a sound and crouches down in hiding. A WOMAN enters, carrying a bundle. Her face is covered by a shroud. She stops, furtively looks around, then lays the bundle down on the ground in front of her. She partially unwraps it, takes a small object from a pouch and places it inside the bundle.

WOMAN: O Artemis, Maiden of the Silver Bow, goddess of childbirth and guardian of children, accept this humble offering and bestow your protection on this child, who through no fault of its own has been judged not fit to live. Please, I beg you!

ARTEMIS stays hidden, watching and listening. The WOMAN starts to hurry away but the baby's piercing cry stops her in her tracks. Her attention is drawn back to the bundle. She starts to move toward it, but resists the impulse, firmly shaking her head "no." The WOMAN exits. ARTEMIS approaches the bundle.

ARTEMIS: Another one. Mortals: they've got a million excuses. "Too many mouths to feed. Not enough inheritance to go around. This one's sickly, that one's deformed." Or it's... *(she unwraps the bundle to look at the baby)* just as I thought — a girl. "Girls are stupid! They bleed! Their dowries are too expensive!" So they leave them out here with tokens — or in this case, *(lifting the object in the bundle to look at it)* half a token. Are they trying to insult me, or are they just really cheap? *(almost tosses the token away, looks down at the baby, tucks it back into the bundle)* Fine, you keep it, little one. For all the good it'll do you. Oh, it makes them feel better. It soothes their guilty consciences. "O Artemis, please watch over my baby." But deep down they know all their prayers don't mean a damn thing. The Fates decide these things, not me. Well, that's not entirely true. I could intervene if I really wanted to. But I don't. Unlike that pathetic bunch of idiots up on Olympus, I'm just not interested in getting caught up in mortals' lives, playing around with their destinies. Not to mention having sex with them at the drop of a hat, like my dear father Zeus. Mortals put their children out to die; Zeus collects them like trophies. One's just as bad as the other, if you ask me. No, I don't need any of them. I live on my own. I hunt what I need. I go my own way.

The baby starts crying again.

ARTEMIS: Sorry, little one. I can't help you. It won't be long now, however it comes: Starvation... Freezing...

She hears a low growling sound.

ARTEMIS: Or maybe it's coming even quicker than that.

ARTEMIS aims her arrow in the direction of the growling. A BEAR enters. She quickly lowers her bow.

ARTEMIS: Of course, even if I wanted to save you, I couldn't shoot an animal that's sacred to me.

ARTEMIS watches as the BEAR goes over and picks up the baby.

ARTEMIS: That's it, little one. I'm afraid you're done for. Too bad.

Artemis turns away, reluctant to look, but instead of tearing into the baby, the BEAR just gazes at it with curiosity.

ARTEMIS: Wait a minute. I smell blood on that bear. She's just eaten. She's not hungry. You're not going to be bear-dinner after all! Lucky baby. Now you can go back to dying a nice, slow death.

Losing interest in the baby, the BEAR moves to drop it. But the baby has latched on to one of the Bear's teats. The Bear tries to tear the baby off, but she hangs on tenaciously. After a few tries the Bear gives up and shuffles away, the baby still hanging from its teat.

ARTEMIS: Now that's something you don't see every day!

Curious, ARTEMIS exits, following the BEAR and the baby.

Act I, Scene 2

Mount Olympus, where all the gods appear in half-mask. The god ZEUS is having a bit of nookie with a NYMPH. Off to one side, ION lounges around playing a game of knucklebones, looking like the ancient Greek equivalent of a couch potato. Off to the other side the god HERMES sits reading. All are rudely interrupted by the entrance of the goddess ATHENE, extremely agitated.

ATHENE: Papa?

ZEUS: Athene?

ATHENE: Papa! Look at them!

ZEUS: Look at who, darling girl?

ZEUS waves the NYMPH away.

ATHENE: Down there! You've got to do something about those people!

ZEUS: What people?

ATHENE: The people in Argenopolis, that scuzzy little polis I told you about. They have a silver mine, papa. A silver mine!

ZEUS: And this is a problem because?

ATHENE: Oh, papa, we already talked about this. Don't you remember? Now that they've got their own silver mine they'll start making their own coins and before you know it they'll be richer than Athens!

ZEUS: Now Athene, don't get yourself all worked up…

ATHENE: Those weaselly little upstarts are going to throw their weight around all over Greece. I just know it! They might even launch an invasion and you can't let that happen, papa! You gave me Athens for my very own and you promised me you would never ever ever let anything bad happen to it.

ZEUS: Yes, sweetheart…

ATHENE: So, would you please send Hermes down there to make sure they don't, please, please, pretty please with an olive on top?

ZEUS: Of course I will. *(to Hermes)* Hermes?

HERMES, who has been listening to the whole exchange with thinly veiled disgust, looks over with weary resignation as his name is called.

HERMES: Yes, father?

ZEUS: I want you to head down to this… What's it called again?

ATHENE: Argenopolis.

ZEUS: Go to Argenopolis and shut down that silver mine.

HERMES: Why? Is Athens the only polis that's allowed to get rich?

ATHENE: That's right, brother. Because it's my polis!

HERMES: And just how am I supposed to go about shutting down this mine?

ATHENE: Who cares? Flood it! Blow it up! Just do it!

HERMES: Right. Blow up the mine. Who cares if we kill thousands of mortals in the process?

ATHENE: Well, duh! They all die sooner or later. Papa, if Hermes is not going to take this seriously then…

HERMES: Okay, okay. Forget I said anything.

ZEUS: You're a smart fellow, son. You'll figure something out.

HERMES: I'm the messenger boy. I don't really have much choice, do I?

ZEUS: And since you're going down there anyway... *(nodding toward ION)* Take this ne'er-do-well along with you.

ION: *(leaping to his feet)* Me?

ZEUS: Yes, you.

ION: Why do I have to go? What'd I do?

ZEUS: Nothing. That's just it. You sit around here playing knucklebones and stuffing your face all day. You're getting to the age where you have to make up your mind. Are you going to live as a god or as a mortal?

ION: Well, I'd call that a no-brainer!

ZEUS: Still, it'd be good for you to see how the other half lives. You're going down.

ION: No, I'm not.

ZEUS: What did you say?

ION: I'm not going.

ZEUS: Ion, I just told you...

ION: And I just told you...

They shout over one another.

ZEUS: You are going to do as I say and get your half-mortal ass down to Argenopolis!

ION: I'm not going down to that hot dusty little town where the animals crap right in the street!

They stare one another down. A stand-off. Finally ZEUS pulls away.

ZEUS: Hermes, you better figure out a way to make him go down there or I am going to be very upset!

HERMES mouths "why-do-I-have-to?" outrage, but says nothing.

ZEUS stomps out, followed by a triumphant, self-satisfied ATHENE.

HERMES: Look, Ion, just humor him, will you?

ION: Why? I already know I want to stay here. Why would I want to be a mortal?

HERMES: Oh, little brother. Immortality is greatly over-rated. Especially when you think of spending eternity with a bunch like this.

ION:	I don't care what he says. I'm not going!
HERMES:	Look at it this way. It'll be a change from the mind-numbing boredom of this place. And you know… there's girls down there.
ION:	Girls?
HERMES:	Lots and lots of beautiful mortal girls. And the best part is that you're not related to any of them. I mean, practically every female in this place is your aunt or half-sister…
ION:	I never thought of that…
HERMES:	So what say we go down and just have a look around?

ION and HERMES descend to the city below.

Act I, Scene 3

The gymnasium at Argenopolis. DIAGORAS spars with CLEON, who is in a mask and pretending to be a slave. The round ends as DIAGORAS gets CLEON in a choke-hold.

CLEON:	Okay, I've had it! Enough!

Startled at the sound of the voice, DIAGORAS releases the hold and springs back.

DIAGORAS:	Excellency!
CLEON:	*(removing his mask, laughing)* I knew you were training hard, but I had no idea you were turning yourself into a lethal weapon!
DIAGORAS:	I'm so sorry. I had no idea… I thought you were a slave!
CLEON:	I had to trick you. If you'd known it was me you would have let me off easy.
DIAGORAS:	How was your trip, sir?
CLEON:	Oh, fine. Except for those fellows in Corinth giving me a hard time, going on and on about how they were going to whip our asses at the Olympiad…
DIAGORAS:	No way! We're going to kick some Corinthian butt!
CLEON:	That's exactly what I told them! Diagoras of Argenopolis is going to bring home that olive crown next month!
DIAGORAS:	I'm going to give it my best shot, sir.
CLEON:	That's my boy. Oh, Diagoras, looking at you right now makes me think of my own son. Iphicles was a fine wrestler.

DIAGORAS:	I know, sir. I use to watch him spar when I was a boy.
CLEON:	He never got his chance to go to the Olympiad…
DIAGORAS:	He gave his life for the polis, sir. I'm honored to even be mentioned in the same breath.
CLEON:	I should be going. Should I send in the slave? The one who was supposed to be sparring with you?
DIAGORAS:	No, that's it for me. I have to meet my father in the agora.
CLEON:	I'll walk with you.

They exit.

Act I, Scene 4

The steps of the Temple at Argenopolis. Two figures enter: HERMES and ION disguised as women — an Oracle and her priestess. ION, as the Oracle, babbles nonsense. HERMES translates for him. Off to one side, BAUCIS observes.

HERMES:	Hear my warning: The white bird foretells a terrible fate for the citizens of Argenopolis.

A white bird (puppet) passes overheard.

ION:	(babble)
HERMES:	My mistress, the Oracle, speaks in a strange tongue that only I understand. I will translate: "The Graeae will have their revenge!"
ION:	(babble)
HERMES:	"The Gray Ones are furious that their sanctuary has been penetrated. Now that their eons-old slumber has been disturbed, even Zeus himself will not be able to stop the destruction that will ensue!"
BAUCIS:	Destruction? Of what?
ION:	(babble)
HERMES:	"Of Argenopolis and all its citizens."
ION:	(babble)
HERMES:	"Even the Fates will not override the Graeae, who are their sisters from the ancient times. There is only one way to appease their anger and that is to stop plundering their domain!"

ION:	*(babble)*
HERMES:	"This means you must shut down your silver mine at once. Then, and only then, may there be a chance that your city will be spared."

ION and HERMES exit, ION screeching.

Act I, Scene 5

The edge of the agora of Argenopolis. PHILEMON is talking to a young student, THYESTES. The slave girl ZOE watches from a distance.

PHILEMON:	Now, Thyestes, tell me again: Why have I kept you after class?
THYESTES:	Because I was playing knucklebones during your lecture, sir.
PHILEMON:	What else?
THYESTES:	Because I didn't do my assignment, sir.
PHILEMON:	And what happens to young men who don't do their assignments and waste time in class?
THYESTES:	They waste their father's money.
PHILEMON:	What else?
THYESTES:	They bring shame on their family's good name.
PHILEMON:	Two correct answers in a row! Well done, Thyestes. Now let's get back to the riddle in that passage you were supposed to memorize: What creature walks on four legs in the morning, two legs in the afternoon and three legs in the evening?
THYESTES:	Let's see... Some animals have four legs, but can walk on two. You know, like a bear...
PHILEMON:	All right, fine. But when have you ever seen an animal walking on three legs?
THYESTES:	Oh! I know! Once I saw a boar that got its leg bitten off in a fight with a wolf. That was neat.
PHILEMON:	And this boar was able to walk on three legs?
THYESTES:	Ah, no, sir. It was dead.
PHILEMON:	Thyestes, what in the name of the gods does a dead boar have to do with the question I posed?

THYESTES:	Ah, nothing, sir. I guess.
PHILEMON:	You guess? Fine, that's enough for today. I expect you to have that passage memorized for tomorrow.
THYESTES:	I will, sir.
PHILEMON:	Well? What's keeping you?
THYESTES:	Thought I might stay around and say hi to Diagoras. I saw his match last week with Polydamas from Thessaly. He whipped that guy's ass!
PHILEMON:	Well, why don't you give him your congratulations some other time?
THYESTES:	Okay, sir. See you tomorrow.
PHILEMON:	*(with deep resignation)* Yes, Thyestes. Till tomorrow.

PHILEMON looks around, as if expecting someone, then seems as though he's preparing to leave, when he hears a small voice.

ZOE:	"Man!"
PHILEMON:	Who's there?

ZOE steps out where PHILEMON can see her.

PHILEMON:	What did you say?
ZOE:	"Man."
PHILEMON:	So you know the answer to the riddle? *(ZOE nods)* Then tell me why the answer is "man"?
ZOE:	Because man crawls on all fours as a baby, walks upright as a young man and carries a cane in old age.
PHILEMON:	Very good. You must have seen "Oedipus the King" by Sophocles of Athens.
ZOE:	No.
PHILEMON:	Then how do you know the riddle of the Sphinx?
ZOE:	I heard you talking to your students.
PHILEMON:	You listen to my lectures?
ZOE:	*(nodding)* When I come to the market, I stay over there.
PHILEMON:	Yes, come to think of it, I have seen you around before. What else have you learned from Sophocles?

ZOE: "It was not Zeus who gave them forth
Nor Justice, dwelling with the Gods below
Who traced these laws for all the sons of men
Nor did I deem thy edicts strong enough
Coming from mortal man, to set at naught
The unwritten laws of God that know not change.
They are not of today nor yesterday."

PHILEMON: Antigone's defiant speech! Most of my students couldn't recite that. What's your name, child?

ZOE: I'm Zoe, of the house of Polydorus.

PHILEMON: Polydorus the Chief Justice? You're very fortunate to serve in such a fine, upstanding household.

ZOE: Yes, I suppose I am.

PHILEMON: Zoe, you should have the opportunity to develop that excellent mind of yours. Perhaps we could arrange for you to attend my classes without hiding behind a pillar? I could speak to Polydorus and…

ZOE: No! Don't! If my mistress finds out she'll beat me for wasting time.

PHILEMON: Wasting time, eh? Unfortunately, you're probably right. Well, then, I want you to keep coming as often as you can, and when class is over, we can talk. It'll just be between you and me. What do you say?

Before ZOE can answer, CLEON and DIAGORAS enter.

CLEON: Ah, there he is. Philemon, my friend!

PHILEMON: Cleon! Welcome home.

CLEON: I've just come from sparring with this boy of yours. He practically took my head off! I can't believe how far he's come in the short time I've been gone.

DIAGORAS: You exaggerate, sir…

CLEON: Not a bit! Philemon, everywhere I went people wanted to talk about the magnificent young wrestler from Argenopolis. It was all I could do to keep their minds on trade matters!

PHILEMON: I thought you weren't expected back for another couple of weeks. I trust there were no problems?

CLEON: Oh, far from it. I've come back with a ton of orders for silver — far more than we can fill. The most pressing thing right now is getting production at the mine back up.

PHILEMON: I see you've wasted no time calling a special assembly for tomorrow.

CLEON: Philemon, even you have to admit that this problem of runaway slaves is a festering sore. We can't put off dealing with it any longer. If we can't fill those orders the polis will just take their business elsewhere.

PHILEMON: I agree with you completely, my friend. The time has come to deal with the matter. I've been giving it a good deal of thought, and I think I may have hit upon the solution.

CLEON: Really? Well, that's certainly good news. There's nothing the polis needs more than…

A commotion offstage. A voice is heard.

VOICE: *(offstage)* Hey! Come back here with that!

A person dressed in the garb of a SHE-BEAR races onstage, carrying a basket of food.

VOICE: Stop her!

CLEON: What the…??

The SHE-BEAR almost gets away, but DIAGORAS pounces on her.

DIAGORAS: Oh no you don't!

Diagoras tries to wrest the food away from her, but she puts up a fierce struggle.

CLEON, PHILEMON and ZOE watch in appalled fascination as DIAGORAS and the SHE-BEAR have a knock-down, drag-out fight. DIAGORAS is shocked to discover he's met his match in physical strength. Finally the SHE-BEAR manages to pull away, grabbing the food as she races offstage.

DIAGORAS: Go on, run! Just wait! We're going to rid the polis of scum like you!

CLEON: Look at that! Smack in the middle of the agora and laughing in our faces while she steals from us! Do you see now, Philemon? This whole business has gotten out of hand. We've got to send a force of hoplites out there and put a stop to it once and for all.

ZOE bursts out, unable to contain herself.

ZOE: You can't!

The others turn to look at her, shocked that a slave girl has spoken up so boldly.

CLEON: Oh really? Why is that?

ZOE: The she-bear is a demi-god under the protection of Artemis!

DIAGORAS: Demi-god? I don't think so!

ZOE:	It's true! She has the strength of a hundred men!
CLEON:	Well, then, you must have the strength of a hundred and one, Diagoras!

CLEON and DIAGORAS share a laugh.

PHILEMON:	How do you know the she-bear is a demi-god?
ZOE:	Everyone says so.
PHILEMON:	I see. And who is this "everyone"? Somebody I know? Is "everyone" a person I can drink wine with at symposium? Child, you must learn to think for yourself, not just regurgitate nonsense you hear from others. Even if their name is "everyone."
DIAGORAS:	What do you expect from a house slave, father? All they do is sit around and gossip all day.

More laughter from CLEON and DIAGORAS.

DIAGORAS:	*(to ZOE)* What are you standing around for anyway? Don't you have marketing to do?

ZOE, embarrassed and intimidated, exits.

PHILEMON:	Come back tomorrow! We'll talk some more about Antigone's speech.
CLEON:	Antigone? I know you choose not to keep slaves in your household, Philemon. But teaching them?
PHILEMON:	That child is hungrier for knowledge than all the rest of my students put together.
CLEON:	Well, nothing you do surprises me anymore, my friend.

During their discussion, DIAGORAS notices something on the ground. He picks it up: a piece of tablet on a chain.

PHILEMON:	What's that?
DIAGORAS:	I don't know. Looks like a broken tablet.
CLEON:	I saw something hanging around her neck. Maybe you pulled it off during the fight.

CLEON puts the chain around DIAGORAS' neck.

CLEON:	There! This'll be your trophy for defeating the great she-bear!

The men laugh. BAUCIS enters, carrying groceries.

PHILEMON:	Ah, there you are, my dear. Let me help you.

CLEON:	Baucis! It's been ages.
BAUCIS:	Hello, Excellency.
CLEON:	Oh, come now. No formalities between old friends.

BAUCIS notices some blood on DIAGORAS' cheek.

BAUCIS:	What happened to you?
DIAGORAS:	Nothing.
BAUCIS:	You're bleeding.
DIAGORAS:	Don't fuss over me!
CLEON:	That she-bear just came barreling through the agora stealing food, but your boy here made short work of her!
BAUCIS:	So that's what all the commotion was about. Everything happened so fast nobody knew what was going on. I thought maybe it had something to do with that Oracle.
CLEON:	Oracle? What Oracle?
BAUCIS:	She was at the temple earlier. She said the Graeae are furious about the mine and unless it's shut down they'll take revenge on the whole polis.
CLEON:	The Graeae! Come on! They're just old hags in stories to frighten children into being good. Who is this Oracle?
BAUCIS:	Nobody knows. But as soon as she opened her mouth a white bird came swooping down from the roof of the temple.
DIAGORAS:	A white bird? That doesn't sound good.
BAUCIS:	People are very upset. Everyone's talking about it.
CLEON:	Why in the world would the gods expect us to abandon the mine, the source of our prosperity? It makes no sense.
PHILEMON:	If an Oracle tells me that this is water under my feet instead of earth, am I supposed to believe it?
BAUCIS:	I have no idea if she's really an Oracle. But I do know that silver mine has brought nothing but trouble to this polis.
DIAGORAS:	Mother, please don't start…
BAUCIS:	It's no wonder the slaves are running away. The foremen work them till they drop dead from exhaustion. If they don't get killed in a cave-in first…

DIAGORAS: Mother! Please pardon my mother, Excellency. She doesn't realize what she's saying...

BAUCIS: I know perfectly well what I'm saying! Conditions in that mine are terrible, and everyone in the polis knows it.

CLEON: It's all right, Diagoras. Baucis is a woman of independent mind. She brings up some very good points.

PHILEMON: Indeed. They're the very points I'll be raising at the assembly, along with my doubts about the wisdom of embarking on military action.

CLEON: Really, Philemon. And what do you suggest we do instead?

PHILEMON: I'm going to propose that we give the runaways the chance to come back voluntarily.

CLEON: Voluntarily? What in the world makes you think they'd do that?

PHILEMON: The prospect of winning their freedom.

CLEON: Their freedom? What, we're supposed to set them all free? Then pray tell who's going to work the mine?

PHILEMON: The slaves will. We give the runaways the chance to earn their freedom — if they agree to come back and work the mine for a specified period of time.

CLEON: Philemon, this would be a very interesting idea to discuss in the symposium, but as a practical measure...

PHILEMON: It's not all that radical an idea, you know. There are all kinds of precedents for freeing slaves: as a reward for bravery or hard work or long service. The only difference here is the numbers. I've been discussing the idea with a good many people in your absence, Cleon. I think the citizens of Argenopolis are ready to try something new.

CLEON: Well, then, I'll look forward to a spirited debate on this at the assembly tomorrow. And we'll see which way the vote goes.

PHILEMON: Oh, no, my friend. The vote can't be held tomorrow. A motion on a military campaign requires three days' notice.

CLEON: Yes, of course. The assembly can always rely on your vast knowledge of democratic procedure, Philemon. Well, there's at least one thing we agree on completely. Why don't you come walk with me through the agora and talk to people so we can correct this nonsense about that Oracle before things get out of hand.

PHILEMON: I'd be glad to. Diagoras, help your mother get those groceries home.

CLEON:	Keep up the training, my boy. See you at the gymnasium!
DIAGORAS:	Yes, sir.

CLEON and PHILEMON exit.

BAUCIS:	*(holds out groceries to a sulky DIAGORAS)* What?
DIAGORAS:	It's bad enough you go to the agora, carting around groceries like a slave. But did you have to go spouting off about the mine?
BAUCIS:	I had something to say.
DIAGORAS:	Women should keep their thoughts to themselves! Sometimes I wonder how I was born into this family.

DIAGORAS angrily exits.

BAUCIS:	Diagoras!

BAUCIS exits.

Act I, Scene 6

ION and HERMES enter, no longer in disguise.

ION:	Okay, explain it to me again: Why did I have to dress up like an old bag and talk gibberish?
HERMES:	I had to make them think you were an Oracle delivering a prophecy.
ION:	And you couldn't come up with something better than that old yarn about the Graeae?
HERMES:	Mortals usually fall for those stories hook, line and sinker.
ION:	Well, they didn't go for the bird omen.
HERMES:	They did at first! Things were going great until those two old guys came along and started telling everybody to ignore us! What are we going to do now?
ION:	Why don't we just go make the mine collapse? Zeus will be happy, Athene will be happy, and we can get out of here.
HERMES:	We can't do that, little brother.
ION:	Why not?
HERMES:	I don't believe in just willy-nilly interfering in mortals' lives.

ION: But you're a god!

HERMES: Yes, but unlike some gods who shall remain nameless I have principles. You see, Ion, the true art of being a god lies in getting mortals to do what you want them to do, while tricking them into thinking it's what they want to do. Besides, it's more fun that way, and since we're stuck here for a while, we might as well have a little fun. Right, little brother?

ION: Why do you keep calling me that? I'm not your brother.

HERMES: I don't know. "Little nephew" just doesn't have the same ring to it.

ION: This is all so unbelievably boring.

HERMES: Quiet. I hear someone coming.

ARTEMIS enters.

ION: Hey, isn't that your sister?

HERMES: Shhh!

ARTEMIS: Did I do the right thing? She had such a strong rage to live. Something in me couldn't let her die.

A tableau, as mask characters act out Artemis' story. The BEAR enters, carrying a young ALECTO.

ARTEMIS: I had the bear suckle her until she grew to be a child. But I knew the day would come when she would have to learn the ways of humans. So the bear took her to a farmhouse on the edge of a village…

The Bear hands the young ALECTO to a FARMING COUPLE. ALECTO lets loose with a terrifying scream. She tries to cling to the BEAR, but the BEAR tears her off.

ARTEMIS: This time she couldn't hang on.

The FARMING COUPLE order her to do chores. Young ALECTO resists. They yell at her and beat her.

ARTEMIS: They treated her like a slave — no, worse — like an animal. They didn't even bother to give her a name. Maybe I should have stepped in to help her, but she had to learn the true nature of humans for herself. And they were never able to break her. I knew they wouldn't be able to, not this one. Finally one day she ran away… Her first night on her own, she lay down to sleep. In a dream I appeared to her and gave her a name, the name of one of the Furies. She woke up the next morning shouting it into the hills:

ARTEMIS&ALECTO:
> Alecto: the Unnameable!

ARTEMIS: From that moment on she knew she could survive on her own. She shunned human society, donned the bear skin and went into the wild where she lived on skinned hares and the herbs of the forest.

ALECTO exits.

ARTEMIS: But as she grew older I watched them coming to her: all the slaves and outlaws wanting to feed off her incredible strength. She tried to turn them away, but no matter. They kept coming and coming. And every day I ask myself: Did I do the right thing, taking her under my protection? Or have I defied the Fates? Was she meant to die? Will she have to pay the price for my keeping her alive?

ALECTO enters, followed at a distance by ZOE. ARTEMIS withdraws and watches them from a distance.

ALECTO: Didn't I tell you to stop following me?

ZOE: Please let me go with you.

ALECTO: I can't look after a kid!

ZOE: I'm not a kid!

ALECTO: Beat it! You'll just drag me down.

ZOE: I can help you. I'll work hard. I learn quickly.

ALECTO: I said go back where you came from.

ZOE: You don't know what it's like there. My master comes to my bed at night and he… I can't go back to that. I saw what you did in the agora. You're stronger than Diagoras, stronger than anyone. That's why all the runaway slaves are coming to you. Please. I'll do anything. I won't go back. I'd rather die.

ALECTO: You really think you can survive out here? It's not the cushy life you had at your master's house.

ZOE: I don't care.

ALECTO: You have to be like a Spartan girl — only tougher.

ZOE: I will. You'll see.

They walk silently a moment.

ALECTO: So. Have you got a name?

ZOE:	It's Zoe.
ALECTO:	Who's this Diagoras you were talking about?
ZOE:	The one you fought with in the agora. He's a champion wrestler.
ALECTO:	That explains why he's so strong. Who were those other people I saw you with?
ZOE:	Philemon. He's a teacher, a good man. And Cleon.
ALECTO:	I take it you don't think he's a good man.
ZOE:	He's the Archon.
ALECTO:	What's that?
ZOE:	The head of the assembly.
ALECTO:	Oh, yeah. The slaves told me about him. He's the one they'd like to shove down the mineshaft. *(feels around her neck)*
ZOE:	What is it?
ALECTO:	Nothing. I think I lost something, that's all.
ZOE:	How much farther is it?
ALECTO:	A ways yet.
ZOE:	Can we stop and rest a minute?
ALECTO:	I warned you. I don't like whiners.

ALECTO & ZOE exit. ARTEMIS follows them at a distance. HERMES and ION emerge from their hiding place.

ION:	Wow! Who is that?
HERMES:	The one they call the she-bear. And her conversation with that little slave girl just told me everything I need to know about the good citizens of Argenopolis. Oh, this is so perfect, little brother. Come on. Let's get going.
ION:	What? Where?
HERMES:	We're going to go see the teacher, what's his name? Philemon.
ION:	Why?
HERMES:	He's got a lot of respect. People listen to him. If I can bring him around, I'll have the whole town in my pocket.

ION:	But he was the one who went around telling people not to listen to us.
HERMES:	Trust me. I've got an idea. Come on, we have to find out where he lives.
ION:	I'd much rather follow her.
HERMES:	Now I see where the story of her being suckled by a bear came from. She must've been put out to die when she was a baby.
ION:	What? You mean mortals abandon their children?
HERMES:	Uh-huh. One of the few ways in which they're not morally superior to the gods.
ION:	Well, if all mortal girls were like her I might reconsider!
HERMES:	I wouldn't get my hopes up if I were you, little brother. She's under my sister Artemis' protection. And you know what that means…
BOTH:	Virginity!
ION:	Bummer!

HERMES and ION exit.

Act I, Scene 7

BAUCIS and DIAGORAS arrive at home. The air is still thick with tension as they put away groceries. BAUCIS notices the chain around his neck.

BAUCIS:	What's this?
DIAGORAS:	Nothing.
BAUCIS:	Where did it come from?
DIAGORAS:	The she-bear.
BAUCIS:	But how did you get it?
DIAGORAS:	I told you. It came off her when we fought in the agora. What's the big deal? Here, *(flings it at her)* take it if you're so interested.
BAUCIS:	Diagoras. There's something we have to talk about.
DIAGORAS:	All right, I was bad, I mouthed off at you in public. I'm sorry. Okay?
BAUCIS:	It's not about that.

DIAGORAS:	Then what?
BAUCIS:	Something your father and I probably should have told you long ago.
DIAGORAS:	What? What's the big mystery?
BAUCIS:	You see that pot over there?
DIAGORAS:	Sure. It's been there as long as I can remember. What about it?
BAUCIS:	There's a reason why we keep it there… It was that pot that brought you to us.
DIAGORAS:	Brought me? What do you mean?
BAUCIS:	There's a spot at the very edge of the agora… People in Argenopolis all know it… If a baby is born and the parents don't wish to raise it, they can leave it there in hopes that someone will find it who does want to raise it. Maybe someone who can't have a child of their own…
DIAGORAS:	So?
BAUCIS:	So they take the baby to this place and leave it in a pot. Like that one.
DIAGORAS:	I have no idea why you're telling me all this.
BAUCIS:	Diagoras. I found you in this pot, on the edge of the agora.
DIAGORAS:	What?
BAUCIS:	You were only a few days old, but I could see you were a beautiful baby, healthy and strong. I brought you home to Philemon. It was the happiest day of our lives!
DIAGORAS:	Are you saying that you're not my mother?
BAUCIS:	I did not give birth to you, no, Diagoras.
DIAGORAS:	Then who did?
BAUCIS:	We don't know.
DIAGORAS:	You never told me any of this?
BAUCIS:	We never meant to deceive you… We were waiting for the right time.
DIAGORAS:	I was left on the edge of the agora?
BAUCIS:	It must have been done out of love, Diagoras. Someone chose that spot because they knew you'd be found right away.
DIAGORAS:	Love? How can you say that? Why would the woman who gave birth to me abandon me? Unless there was a sort of curse on my birth?

BAUCIS:	No, Diagoras, I was the one who was cursed. We tried for years to have a child. But then we found you. You were our gift from the twenty-seven gods!
DIAGORAS:	I have no lineage. I'm nobody. Worse than nobody.
BAUCIS:	That's not true. You're our son!
DIAGORAS:	No I'm not! All these years I thought I knew who I was, but I'm just some foundling you took in like a stray animal!
BAUCIS:	No, we loved you and raised you as our own flesh and blood.
DIAGORAS:	I could be a child of slaves for all you know! Do you see what this means? I'll be barred from competing in the Olympiad.
BAUCIS:	No, that won't happen. No one in the polis knows.
DIAGORAS:	What do you mean? How could they not know?
BAUCIS:	After we found you, I stayed in seclusion for several months. We simply told people that the gods had finally blessed us with a child. No one in Argenopolis had any reason to suspect anything different. But now I'm not so sure of… *(holding out one of the objects)* I always wondered why it was broken.

BAUCIS holds up the other object. They form two halves of a tablet.

DIAGORAS:	Stop talking in riddles. You're driving me crazy!
BAUCIS:	This girl, Diagoras. The one they call the she-bear. Did you notice anything about her?
DIAGORAS:	What do you mean, did I notice anything?
BAUCIS:	How old was she, would you say?
DIAGORAS:	I don't know!
BAUCIS:	Near your own age?
DIAGORAS:	I suppose. Why? What difference does it make?
BAUCIS:	This was wrapped up with you when we found you. And this… *(holds up the other piece)* you got from the bear-girl. See? It's a likeness of Artemis and her bow. Together they form one piece.

DIAGORAS takes the tablet from BAUCIS. A pause as the gist of what she's saying slowly dawns on him.

DIAGORAS:	But even if… I don't understand. You found me. What about her?
CLEON:	If the story they tell about her is true, she was put out to die.

DIAGORAS:	But why? Why her and not me?
BAUCIS:	Because you're a boy, Diagoras. That's why they left you where they knew you'd be found.
DIAGORAS:	I can't listen to any more of this!
BAUCIS:	Where are you going?
DIAGORAS:	I don't know.
BAUCIS:	Please don't go.
DIAGORAS:	*(throwing her off)* Leave me alone.
BAUCIS:	Diagoras!

PHILEMON enters. DIAGORAS almost knocks him over on his way out.

PHILEMON:	What's going on!
DIAGORAS:	You're not my mother! And you're not my father!

DIAGORAS exits.

PHILEMON:	What have you gone and done?
BAUCIS:	I had to tell him, Philemon.
PHILEMON:	How could you do such a thing?
BAUCIS:	He was going to find out sooner or later!
PHILEMON:	Where's he going?
BAUCIS:	I don't know.
PHILEMON:	Diagoras! You come back here right now.

Act I, Scene 8

DIAGORAS enters, out of breath, in a state of extreme agitation. He comes to a cliff, looks over the edge.

DIAGORAS:	Why not? You're worse than an animal. You have nothing left to live for.

Diagoras stands up, poised to jump. ALECTO enters, sees DIAGORAS. She sneaks up from behind and pulls him away from the edge of the cliff. They struggle, until she finally pins him down.

DIAGORAS:	Leave me alone!

ALECTO: What? Are you crazy? Hey — you're that wrestler, Diagoras.

DIAGORAS: I said go away and leave me alone!

ALECTO: Your arm's bleeding.

ALECTO looks around, picks a leaf from a nearby plant, rubs it on his arm.

DIAGORAS: What's that?

ALECTO: Henbane

DIAGORAS: Ouch.

ALECTO: So the wrestler-boy isn't so tough!

DIAGORAS: What's it do?

ALECTO: Slows down the bleeding.

DIAGORAS: How do you know?

ALECTO: You learn a few things living out here. So what do you want to do a stupid thing like that for? Don't you want to live?

DIAGORAS: Maybe not.

ALECTO: Feeling sorry for yourself, eh? What happened? Did you lose a wrestling match?

DIAGORAS: You think you know all about me, don't you?

ALECTO: I know you're a pampered little boy who's had everything given to you on a silver platter.

DIAGORAS: Maybe there are a few things about me you don't know.

ALECTO: I'm sure I wouldn't be interested. There, that should stop it up so you won't bleed to death on the way home.

DIAGORAS: I'm not going home.

ALECTO: Why not?

DIAGORAS: Like you said, you wouldn't be interested.

ALECTO: Have it your way. I'm out of here.

ALECTO starts to leave.

DIAGORAS: Hold on.

ALECTO: What?

DIAGORAS: People in Argenopolis are really ticked off at you, you know.

ALECTO: So what else is new?

DIAGORAS: No, it's serious this time. There's a crackdown coming. They're fed up with all the slaves running away. They're planning to send a force of hoplites to raid your hideout.

ALECTO: They'll have to find it first.

DIAGORAS: They will eventually.

ALECTO: Let them come. I'll be long gone before they get there.

DIAGORAS: But what about the slaves?

ALECTO: It's their fight, not mine.

DIAGORAS: They won't stand a chance against all those soldiers.

ALECTO: That's their problem.

DIAGORAS: I thought you were their leader.

ALECTO: Look, wrestler-boy. I never chose to be leader of anything. I live on my own. I look after myself. Nobody ever helped me and I don't expect them to. I told the slaves I'd teach them how to survive out here, and that's it. I don't go out on a limb for anybody.

DIAGORAS: Well, maybe you should care what happens to them!

ALECTO: It doesn't matter whether I care or not! If the soldiers come, that's it, game over. I can't help them.

DIAGORAS: Listen to me. My father has a plan to help the slaves. He's going to put it to the assembly tomorrow.

ALECTO: What are you talking about?

DIAGORAS: All you show up during the assembly tomorrow and tell them the runaways will surrender…

ALECTO: Oh, right!

DIAGORAS: Let me finish! My father is trying to persuade the assembly to let the slaves work for their freedom — if they go back and work in the mine voluntarily…

ALECTO: Right, go back to the hellhole they just escaped from!

DIAGORAS: It might sound crazy to you, but my father's the most respected member of the assembly. People listen to him. And Cleon can't make a move unless the assembly's behind him.

ALECTO: If you think the good citizens of Argenopolis would go for that, you're even stupider than I thought.

They exit, still arguing.

Act I, Scene 9

The cottage, later that day. PHILEMON and BAUCIS sit at the table, deeply bereft.

BAUCIS: I was wrong to tell him. Why was I so stupid?

PHILEMON: Don't berate yourself. Maybe we should have told him sooner. It's never made sense to me, this obsession with blood and lineage. Why should it matter who gave birth to a child, as long as it's loved and cared for?

A sound outside the cottage.

BAUCIS: *(leaping to her feet)* Praise the gods! He's come back!

She races to the door and opens it. HERMES and ION are there.

HERMES: Excuse us. We saw your light and wondered if we might stop and rest a bit

BAUCIS: Oh.

HERMES: We don't want to trouble you…

PHILEMON: No, please, come in, make yourselves comfortable.

BAUCIS: Yes, of course, do come in.

HERMES: We'll only stay a short while.

BAUCIS: It's all right. Please, sit down.

PHILEMON: We were just about to have supper.

ION: Great. I'm starving.

BAUCIS: I'm afraid we don't have much, but you're welcome to share what we have.

HERMES: Thank you…?

BAUCIS: Baucis. My husband's name is Philemon.

ION: My name's Ion and he's Her… maphrodiocles.

PHILEMON: An unusual name. Have you come far?

ION: Oh, quite far.

HERMES: From a little place up north. You wouldn't have heard of it.

PHILEMON: What brings you to this part of Greece?

HERMES: We're… Merchants. We've come to Argenopolis to explore a business opportunity.

PHILEMON:	Well, you've come to the right place. People in Argenopolis are certainly keen on making money.
HERMES:	So I've heard. And what do you do?
PHILEMON:	I'm a teacher.
HERMES:	Ah, a worthy profession. But not exactly a ticket to wealth, is it? Say... I don't know why I didn't think of it earlier. Ion, these people are just the kind of potential investors we're looking for.
PHILEMON:	Investors?
HERMES:	How would you like to get in on the ground floor of a fantastic, once-in-a-lifetime opportunity? Here's how it works: my friend Ion and I are part of a consortium that's buying up olive groves all over Greece. We're going to corner the market. We'll be producing and bottling it in such massive quantities that the Sicilians, the Scythians, the Egyptians — they'll all have to come to us for their oil.
PHILEMON:	But we have only a small olive grove...
HERMES:	I'm not interested in your little olive grove, my good man. I'm talking about shares. I'm offering you the chance to buy shares in this new venture. It's a can't-miss proposition.
PHILEMON:	Shares? I'm not sure I understand. What does all this have to do with making money?
HERMES:	What? Silver coins? Nothing but a fad. They'll be totally obsolete in a few years, just like barter in the old days. You know, I trade you a barrel of my wine for a bushel of your lemons. I mean, come on. That's not how you create wealth. Shares. Investments. Economies of scale. That's the way of the future. I'm telling you, Argenopolis might as well shut down that mine right now. The market for silver is going to take a nosedive, and the mine will become a millstone around this town's neck. Mark my words. Now, what do you say? Shall I count you in?
PHILEMON:	I don't think we're interested.
HERMES:	What? Are you against prosperity?
PHILEMON:	No, but prosperity always comes with a price.
HERMES:	What kind of price?
BAUCIS:	A human cost. That mine has been nothing but trouble for our polis. We used to care about how we treated one another. Now it's torn us apart.

ION: All the more reason to shut it down! Am I right?

PHILEMON: Closing the mine seems to be the theme of the day. Like earlier, in the agora. Some old woman claiming she was an Oracle was carrying on about how the gods have it in for Argenopolis because of the mine. She put the whole town in a panic

HERMES: You think the prophecy was a false one?

PHILEMON: I don't have much use for prophecies. I think we fall back on divine explanations for things that are better explained by reason. If we'd just recognize that the gods are irrelevant to our lives we'd be better off…

ION: Irrelevant? How can you say that?

HERMES: *(interrupting ION)* I'm thirsty tonight. May I have some more milk, please?

BAUCIS: *(looking in the jug)* That's strange. I could have sworn it was almost empty…

HERMES: Thank you, good lady. Do you share your husband's skepticism?

BAUCIS: Not completely. But I do share his opinion that human beings should be responsible to one another, not subject to the whim of the gods.

HERMES: You think the gods govern by whim?

BAUCIS: Sometimes they're like a bunch of selfish children. They play with us like toys and ignore the suffering they cause.

ION: That's blasphemy!

HERMES: Mind your manners, Ion. These people are our gracious hosts. May I have still more of that wonderful milk?

BAUCIS: Like I said, we weren't expecting to have… *(looking in the pitcher)* Oh. There's quite a bit more left. *(pours)*

HERMES: It sounds like the gods have let you down, good lady.

BAUCIS: It's true. The gods haven't been kind to us lately.

HERMES: I'm sorry to hear that. What happened?

PHILEMON: We had a terrible quarrel with our son. He's left us.

HERMES: Quarrels happen all the time in families. He'll be back soon.

BAUCIS: I'm not so sure…

BAUCIS begins to weep softly.

HERMES: Whatever your quarrel was about, I pray the gods will help you heal it. I know they will.

HERMES picks up the pitcher and pours milk into his cup.

HERMES: *(to ION)* More milk, my friend? *(pouring as ION nods eagerly)* Now you both have some more.

PHILEMON: Are you mocking us?

HERMES: Not at all.

PHILEMON: You can see for yourself there's none left.

HERMES: *(looking in the jug)* What I see in here is an abundance of fresh milk.

BAUCIS looks at HERMES strangely. He pours milk in both their cups. She silently and deliberately drains her cup of milk and sets it back down on the table.

HERMES: Here, have some more.

He pours yet more milk in Baucis' cup.

BAUCIS: These men aren't merchants. Are you?

HERMES: No. And I'm afraid… We're not men either.

HERMES shrugs and takes out his staff.

BAUCIS: Divine Hermes?

BAUCIS and PHILEMON stand up, ready to drop to their knees.

HERMES: No, no, no, no, no. No kneeling! Believe me, I'm the one who should be bowing down to you. You have no idea how wonderful it is to actually meet people with some original thoughts in their heads! People you can have a real conversation with!

PHILEMON: But why…? What brings you here?

HERMES: We've been sent down to deliver a warning to the citizens of Argenopolis, and let me tell you, people like you are the only thing that make this dusty little town worth saving!

PHILEMON: Then the prophecy about the mine is true?

HERMES: Well… Yes and no.

BAUCIS: What do you mean?

HERMES: Oh, there's going to be trouble in the mine, all right. But it's got nothing to do with the Graeae. You're absolutely right: most of the

	gods are petty, spoiled, spiteful creatures, like my sister Athene. She's furious that your polis is threatening the supremacy of her precious Athens. So to appease his little darling, Zeus sent me to try and convince you people to abandon the mine.
PHILEMON:	Persuade people to give up the very thing that's made them wealthy? Do you have any idea what you're asking?
HERMES:	But you said yourself the mine's brought nothing but trouble…
PHILEMON:	Much as I don't like the mine, I don't want to see it destroyed by some god's whim. I think we should find human solutions to our problems.
BAUCIS:	Besides, why do you think you can just waltz in here and expect us to do your dirty work for you?
ION:	How dare you talk to a god that way?
HERMES:	No, she's right. I apologize for that stupid ruse about the olive consortium. I just don't know what else to do now.
BAUCIS:	Why don't you try standing up for what you believe in? If you think Zeus and Athene are being cruel and unjust, then refuse be a party to it.
ION:	What can we do? Zeus is king of the gods!
HERMES:	No, once again, you're right, dear lady. It's true I don't have a lot of sway over what happens on Olympus. But maybe it's time I stopped being Zeus' little messenger boy. Ion, we're going back to Olympus. I'm going to tell Athene to back off and leave these people alone. And if Zeus doesn't like it he can shove one of those thunderbolts up his ass!
ION:	Are you out of your mind?
HERMES:	No, little brother. For the first time in eons my head is completely clear. *(to BAUCIS and PHILEMON)* I have you two to thank for that. Now before we go, I want to give you something. What can I do to make your lives a bit easier? More animals? How about a larger olive grove?
BAUCIS:	There's only one thing you can do for us.
HERMES:	What?
BAUCIS:	Find our son Diagoras. Watch out for him, make sure he's safe.
HERMES:	Don't worry. I won't let anything happen to him. You have my sacred word.

ION and HERMES exit.

Act I, Scene 10

At the hideout. DIAGORAS and ALECTO enter, still arguing.

DIAGORAS: That's where you're wrong. Argenopolis is a democracy. Everything important gets decided in the assembly. My father's a brilliant speaker, he can sway people to his point of view…

ALECTO: I don't trust words. I hate words.

DIAGORAS: You haven't seen my father in action. I'm telling you, if you walk into that assembly with me tomorrow, it'll add the element of surprise. They'll be putty in his hands. Now if you'd just stop being so pigheaded and listen!

ZOE enters, carrying a pot of food.

ZOE: Good, you're back. See? I know how to cook nettles so they don't sting… *(she notices DIAGORAS)* Oh.

DIAGORAS: I saw you in the agora earlier.

ZOE shrinks back, terrified.

ALECTO: *(to ZOE)* Don't worry. Nobody knows you're here. I found him alone out on the cliffs.

DIAGORAS: What's she doing here?

ALECTO: She followed me here. Just like you.

DIAGORAS: You should go back home.

ALECTO: Just leave her alone.

DIAGORAS: It's one thing for the mine slaves to run away. But what's she got to complain about? She lives in a nice house. Her master's Polydorus, the most prominent magistrate in the polis.

ALECTO: Yeah, well he's also a creep.

DIAGORAS: What do you know about him?

ALECTO: I know he uses his slave girls as playthings, and the younger they are the better. That's why she ran away.

DIAGORAS: Polydorus? That's not possible.

ALECTO: Isn't it?

DIAGORAS: She's lying.

ALECTO: Then why would she risk her life to come all the way out here?

DIAGORAS:	Well, if it is true, he'll be punished.
ALECTO:	Yeah, right!
DIAGORAS:	It's against the law. He'll be brought before the citizen court. He might even be banished from the polis for life.
ALECTO:	You're a baby. You don't know anything about life.
DIAGORAS:	Maybe I know a few things you don't.
ALECTO:	Even if she did come forward, who'd believe her? You didn't.
DIAGORAS:	*(to ZOE)* Is it true? Did Polydorus really do those things to you?
ZOE:	*(deeply embarrassed, nodding)* Others, too.
DIAGORAS:	Would the other girls be willing to come tell the court?
ZOE:	I don't know.
DIAGORAS:	If the court finds Polydorus guilty, you could be granted your freedom.
ZOE:	My freedom? Really?
ALECTO:	That's ridiculous.
DIAGORAS:	It's true. When a master's guilty of abuse, he has to make reparations by freeing the slave.
ALECTO:	What good would that do Zoe? She's just a kid. She can't live on her own.
DIAGORAS:	I saw you talking to my father, Zoe. He and my mother would take you in until you come of age.
ALECTO:	Don't listen to him, Zoe. He's filling your head with a lot of garbage.
DIAGORAS:	Why is it so hard for you to believe that there are a few good people in this world?
ALECTO:	There isn't one good person in that stinking town of yours.
DIAGORAS:	My parents are!
ALECTO:	If they're so good then why don't you go back to your nice little home?
DIAGORAS:	I will. And you should let me take Zoe back with me so Polydorus can be brought to justice and she can have a decent life.
ALECTO:	I don't want to talk about this anymore!

ALECTO stomps off.

Act I, Scene 11

ION and HERMES enter.

ION:	I have to admit it was cool, that thing you did with the milk jug.
HERMES:	Nothing but a godly parlor trick. I'm ashamed I actually stooped to using it on those people. Maybe the old man's right. Maybe the gods are irrelevant.
ION:	Huh?
HERMES:	Don't you ever wonder about things, little brother? Like, maybe the gods only exist because mortals think we do. They think we're so powerful. But maybe our powers come from the fact that all these mortals believe in them.
ION:	As usual, I have absolutely no idea what you're talking about.

ALECTO, DIAGORAS and ZOE enter.

HERMES:	Shhh!
ION:	It's her! I like her way better without all that bear fur on!

HERMES and ION stay back, unseen by the others.

ZOE:	I'm not sure I want to do this anymore.
DIAGORAS:	But we talked about all that, Zoe. Don't you want your freedom?
ZOE:	I'd rather stay with Alecto.
ALECTO:	He's right, Zoe. It's better this way.
ZOE:	What if they don't believe me? What if they send me back?
ALECTO:	They won't send you back, Zoe. I promise you.
DIAGORAS:	Let's stop and rest a bit.
ALECTO:	You were the one who said we had to get there by dawn.
DIAGORAS:	You can keep going till you drop from exhaustion. I'm taking a break.
ALECTO:	Oh, fine. *(aside, so ZOE can't hear)* I still can't believe I let you talk me into this.
DIAGORAS:	So is all that true? You were raised by a bear?
ALECTO:	How would I know? I was a baby.
DIAGORAS:	How'd you learn to talk?

ALECTO:	From the farmers who took me in.
DIAGORAS:	You lived with some farmers?
ALECTO:	If you can call it living. I was their slave. Till I got fed up with the beatings and ran away.
DIAGORAS:	Don't you ever wonder about your real family?
ALECTO:	No!
DIAGORAS:	You've got a mother out there somewhere…
ALECTO:	The bear was the only mother I ever had. Come on, let's get going.

ALECTO, DIAGORAS, ZOE exit.

HERMES:	That must be him. Their son. I told those nice people I'd keep an eye on him.
ION:	Can't you do that from Olympus?
HERMES:	I think we should stick around a bit longer.
ION:	Have you got a thing for him? That's it. You do, don't you?
HERMES:	He's cute, I admit it. But that doesn't mean I'm going to act on it. I'm not like your father Apollo, who can't keep his hands off mortals. Come on. Let's catch up with them.
ION:	Who'll we tell them we are?
HERMES:	Leave that to me.

HERMES and ION exit.

Act I, Scene 12

DIAGORAS, ALECTO and ZOE enter. HERMES and ION approach them.

HERMES:	Hail, friends!
ALECTO:	Who's there?
HERMES:	Can you tell me if we're on the right road? We're trying to get to Argenopolis.
DIAGORAS:	This is the way.
HERMES:	Are you on your way there too?

ALECTO tries to stop DIAGORAS from answering.

DIAGORAS:	Yes.
HERMES:	Mind if we join you?
DIAGORAS:	No, not at all…
ALECTO:	Ah, we're not really looking for company right now.
DIAGORAS:	Let them come along. What's the harm?
ALECTO:	Where are you from?
HERMES:	Thebes.
ALECTO:	What are you doing in these parts?
HERMES:	My friend and I have run away from our master. We heard there was a band of slaves living outside Argenopolis led by a girl known as the she-bear.
ALECTO:	Why are you looking for her?
HERMES:	We want to join up with her.
DIAGORAS:	Well, look no further.
HERMES:	You're the she-bear?
DIAGORAS:	The very same. *(responding to ALECTO's look of annoyance)* What? They're on our side. *(to HERMES and ION)* You picked a good time to run away, my friend. We're off to the assembly to negotiate a deal for the runaways.
HERMES:	Deal? What kind of deal?
DIAGORAS:	It's my father, Philemon's, idea. If the slaves surrender voluntarily and agree to go back and work in the mine, they'll eventually be able to win their freedom.
HERMES:	Since when do magistrates negotiate with slaves?
DIAGORAS:	Oh, me? I'm not a slave. My name is Diagoras. I'm competing for Argenopolis at the Olympiad.
HERMES:	Diagoras, the famous wrestler?
DIAGORAS:	Have they heard of me in Thebes?
HERMES:	Oh, yes. I'm so honored to meet you.
DIAGORAS:	And you are…?
HERMES:	Ah, Quicksilver. And my friend here is called Ion.

DIAGORAS:	Quicksilver. That's an odd name.
HERMES:	Oh, it's an old name from Crete.
ALECTO:	I thought you were from Thebes.
DIAGORAS:	*(to ALECTO)* Don't be so suspicious.
HERMES:	My mother was originally from Crete. So can we join you?
ALECTO:	Fine. But when we get to Argenopolis keep your distance. We want to do this on our own. And no matter what my friend here says I'm not the leader of anything.
HERMES:	This plan of yours — you honestly think it's going to work?
ALECTO:	Not really.

DIAGORAS shoots a look of annoyance at ALECTO.

HERMES:	I hear the chief magistrate of Argenopolis is one tough customer.
DIAGORAS:	Oh, don't worry about Cleon. He practically treats me like a son. Anyway, he can't do anything without the approval of the assembly. Argenopolis is a real democracy, just like Athens. You'll see when we get there.

DIAGORAS and HERMES walk on ahead.

ION:	So you're the one they call the she-bear.
ALECTO:	Some people call me that.
ION:	Is it true you're under the protection of Artemis?
ALECTO:	How would I know? I don't have a pipeline to the gods.
ION:	So it might not be true, then?
ALECTO:	Maybe. Maybe not. People say a lot of strange things about me.
ION:	Yeah. But I hadn't heard that you were beautiful, too.

ALECTO glowers at ION.

ION:	Does the she-bear have a name?
ALECTO:	Yeah.
ION:	Can I find out what it is?
ALECTO:	Alecto.
ION:	Whoa… Your family named you after one of the Furies?
ALECTO:	I don't have a family.

ION:	Oh, you gave birth to yourself then?
ALECTO:	I might as well have.
ION:	Then you're an even more remarkable creature than they say.

They exit.

Act I, Scene 13

ARTEMIS is alone, looking out on the gathered assembly. CLEON enters.

ARTEMIS: I don't like the look of this.

She watches as HERMES and ION enter. They also watch the action from hiding.

ARTEMIS: Those two… I could swear that's my brother Hermes. And the young fellow looks like he could be one of my nephews. Hard to keep all of Apollo's offspring straight. What are they doing here, passing for mortals?

CLEON: I declare this assembly open. Fellow Citizens: ten years ago Argenopolis was little more than a village compared to the great centers like Athens, Thebes and Corinth. Then the great vein of silver was discovered, the mine opened up and things began to change. As you all know, I've just come back from an important trade mission to northern Greece and the Black Sea, where I was able to lay the groundwork for many new trading partnerships. I don't need to tell you that Argenopolis is poised at a critical juncture in our history. With the growing use of coins, the demand for silver is at unprecedented levels everywhere in this part of the world. The only thing standing in the way of great wealth for our polis is our ability to get that silver out of the ground fast enough.

But we have a problem: With every passing day, production is plummeting as more and more of our slaves run off to join that gang in the mountains. Our economic future hinges on getting the mine working at full capacity again. Now, we can do nothing, and slide back into the economic stagnation of ten years ago. Or we could go down and work the mine ourselves, like the Spartans do, and, to be perfectly honest, some of you fellows look like you could do with a bit of exercise. But I don't think you're ready to sleep on beds of thistle like the Spartans.

I'm asking the assembly for authority to mount a military campaign to scour the mountains until we find that hideout, round those slaves up and bring them back. The silver mine is the path by which

Argenopolis can fulfill its destiny to become the major power in all Greece. I challenge you: Do not let this opportunity slip through our grasp. I'll now take deputations from members of the assembly.

PHILEMON comes forward from the audience onto the playing area.

PHILEMON: My friends, our Chief Magistrate is well spoken, and his proposal has the best interests of the polis at heart. But I see one small problem with it: it won't work. These runaway slaves have had a taste of freedom, and the wise man knows just how difficult it can be to keep the bird in its cage once it's flown free. We can round them up and bring them back, but they'll just run away again. We're not the only polis with this problem; after all, Athens has the same trouble with the slaves in the silver mines at Laureum.

I want us to consider a different solution, a way to bring the runaways back that uses the carrot — so to speak — instead of the stick. I propose we send not a military detachment, but an emissary to deliver the following message. Argenopolis will give the slaves the chance to return of their own free will, on the understanding that if they work the mine diligently for a specified period of time, they will earn their freedom. Mining is back-breaking, perilous work, and there's nothing we can do about that. But the reward for enduring the dangers of mine work should be the promise of freedom. With an incentive like that, those slaves will work that mine ten times harder than they ever did, I promise you. And the future wealth and glory of Argenopolis will be assured.

My good friend Cleon says that wealth is the path to greatness. But I believe that ideas are what will make us great. Democracy only came into being because people were willing to do things in a different way, things that hadn't been tried before. This is an opportunity for Argenopolis to take a bold, visionary step, to lead the way, not only in wealth and political influence, but in the administration of justice itself.

HERMES: *(aside, to ION)* Wow. What a speaker. They just might go for it.

ION: What do you care? The mine'll still be open.

HERMES: He's right, damn it. I'm such a wimp! I swear as soon as this is over I'm going back and telling Zeus there's no good reason why these people shouldn't have their own mine as long as they use it right and don't kill all those poor slaves in the process. Not that Zeus cares about things like that.

CLEON again steps forward to address the audience.

CLEON: My friend Philemon is a brilliant orator. He speaks to the best part of ourselves and challenges us to live up to our ideals. But we've seen what's happened in other polis where slaves have banded together in open revolt against their masters. It is absolutely imperative that we deal with the situation swiftly and firmly, from a position of strength, before it gets out of hand. Now, are there others who wish to speak?

PHILEMON steps forward.

CLEON: Philemon, you've had your say!

PHILEMON: I'm entitled to a final rebuttal. *(to the assembly)* I know many of you agree with Cleon that decisive military action is the best plan. But I must ask you: haven't we had enough evidence to the contrary? Do I need to remind you of the terrible loss of life that Argenopolis suffered in the Thracian campaign? Have we learned nothing from that wrenching experience? We convinced ourselves that there was no risk involved, and the result was that we lost some of our finest young men, including Cleon's own sons Iphicles and Leander. I'm speaking selfishly here. My own son is nearly of age for military service. I can't bear the thought that I might lose him. Surely military action should be our last resort, not the first thing we turn to. I implore you all, as fathers, to do everything in our power to avoid unnecessary bloodshed and give the way of peace — and justice — a chance.

CLEON: Thank you, Philemon. Any other speakers before I call the vote?

The voice of Diagoras rises up from the audience.

DIAGORAS: Yes.

ALECTO, DIAGORAS and ZOE come forward from the audience.

DIAGORAS: We have something to say.

PHILEMON: Diagoras!

CLEON: Diagoras! You brought her in on your own! Good work, my boy!

DIAGORAS: No, sir. You misunderstand. Alecto's here of her own free will.

CLEON: Alecto?

DIAGORAS: Yes, sir. That's the name my… the she-bear is known by.

CLEON: What are you talking about?

DIAGORAS: *(to the assembly)* Alecto the she-bear is my friend. I owe her my life. She's come here with me to tell you that she's ready to stop her thieving ways, and that the runaway slaves are willing to go back to work in the mine in exchange for their freedom, as my father has proposed.

PHILEMON: Is this true? You've agreed to it?

ALECTO nods hesitantly.

PHILEMON: We can put everything in writing. It'll be a legally binding contract.

ALECTO: How do I know you'll honor it?

PHILEMON: The court of the polis will see that it's enforced. Isn't that true, Cleon?

CLEON: If that's the will of the people, I'm obliged to carry it out.

ALECTO: Then I have a condition for your contract.

CLEON: Oh, really? What condition?

ALECTO gestures to ZOE.

ALECTO: This girl's master was using her to satisfy his own needs, unknown to his wife and the rest of the household. I demand that she not be sent back to him. That she be given her freedom. Until she's of age you have to find another home for her, a real home.

DIAGORAS: We will, won't we, father? My mother would be glad to take her in.

CLEON: But she's from the house of Polydorus. Are we going to take the word of a runaway slave over his?

PHILEMON: If what she says is true this child had no choice but to run away. An accusation has been made. We have to follow due process. The penalty for this type of mistreatment is serious. Possible banishment.

CLEON: Banishment? Of our chief justice?

PHILEMON: If Polydorus is found guilty, justice demands that he be dealt with like any other citizen.

ALECTO: Enough talk! Are you going to put it in your contract or not?

CLEON: If the assembly agrees to it, I won't have any choice in the matter.

ALECTO: Then take a vote, right now.

CLEON: Hold on. There's a procedure to be followed here. I'll agree to put Philemon's proposal, with all your conditions, to the assembly for a vote. As soon as you tell me where your hideout is.

ALECTO: No!

CLEON: Come on, I've given ground. You have to make a show of good faith too.

ALECTO: You don't need to know! When the vote's passed I'll send word. They'll come on their own.

CLEON: How do I know you'll keep your part of the bargain?

DIAGORAS: Come on, Alecto. He's agreed to everything, right here in front of the whole assembly.

CLEON: So. Where's the hideout?

DIAGORAS opens his mouth to speak.

ALECTO: No, don't!

DIAGORAS: It's okay, Alecto. *(to CLEON)* It's in the hills on the road to Megara.

CLEON: Thank you, Diagoras.

CLEON gestures to guards offstage.

CLEON: Arrest her.

DIAGORAS: What… What are you doing?

CLEON: You didn't really think I was going to bargain with lawbreakers, did you?

DIAGORAS: There's hoplites everywhere. We're surrounded.

PHILEMON: You planned this all along.

CLEON: I believe in preparing for every eventuality.

ALECTO: I told you not to tell him!

DIAGORAS: He can't do this!

ALECTO: I should never have listened to you!

PHILEMON: Cleon, this has to be put to the assembly for a vote.

CLEON: There will be no vote!

PHILEMON: On what grounds?

CLEON: My authority as chief magistrate.

PHILEMON: But the will of the assembly is supreme.

CLEON: Then I hereby suspend this assembly.

PHILEMON: You can't do that!

CLEON: Oh? Just watch me.

ION: *(to HERMES)* What do we do?

HERMES: *(to ION)* I don't know.

PHILEMON: Citizens of Argenopolis, are we going to stand by and watch the will of the assembly be cast aside like this? Show of hands, right now, to protest this tyranny!

CLEON:	Be careful, Philemon, or I'll have you arrested too.
DIAGORAS:	For what?
CLEON:	For advocating sedition.
PHILEMON:	That's ridiculous! I expressed an opinion. I'm exercising my rights as a citizen. That's not sedition.
CLEON:	It is when you openly encourage people to defy my authority.
PHILEMON:	Fine. Go ahead, charge me with anything you want. I'll be fully vindicated at my trial. Unless you're thinking of trying to deny me that right, too.
CLEON:	You'll get a trial. But in the meantime you'll go the mines with the rest of them.
DIAGORAS:	No! He's too frail.
CLEON:	He should have thought of that before making incendiary statements.
ION:	*(to HERMES)* Come on, you're a god. Can't you do something?
HERMES:	*(to ION)* No.
ION:	What's wrong?
HERMES:	I don't know. Come on. We better get out of here before somebody notices us.

HERMES and ION exit.

DIAGORAS:	What's the matter with you? You're free men. Don't listen to him.
CLEON:	Silence, Diagoras. Please don't make me arrest you, too.
DIAGORAS:	Go ahead. I dare you! I always used to defend you! Now I see exactly what my father's talking about.
CLEON:	Look at the great demi-god she-bear now.
ALECTO:	Run, Zoe!

ZOE flees the stage. ARTEMIS watches helplessly as ALECTO runs off to try to rescue ZOE.

CLEON:	Return the girl to her master's house.
ALECTO:	No!!!

Offstage scream as ZOE is captured.

END OF ACT I

Act II, Scene 1

Mount Olympus. ARTEMIS enters. Below, in the silver mine, ALECTO, DIAGORAS, HERMES, ION and PHILEMON are working in chains.

ARTEMIS: Athene? Athene! Get out here!

ATHENE enters.

ATHENE: Well, if it isn't my big sister Artemis, on one of her all-too-rare visits to Olympus.

ARTEMIS: Athene, what have you been up to?

ATHENE: Me? Well, let's see, I just did my nails, and earlier I had lunch with Hera…

ARTEMIS: Don't pretend you don't know what I'm talking about! You've been messing with my powers, haven't you?

ATHENE:`   Oh, please. Your pathetic powers? Like I really care about running around shooting arrows.

ARTEMIS: Damn it! Tell me!

ATHENE: Oh, all right. I did make Hermes' powers… dip a little. It must have spilled over onto yours.

ARTEMIS: Hermes? Why?

ATHENE: Because he wasn't doing what he was supposed to! Papa sent him down there with specific orders to get rid of that stupid mine in Argenopolis and instead he's running all over the countryside yakking about how he wants to help the poor, pathetic mortals. I figure if he loves them so much, let him try living like one for awhile.

ARTEMIS: Well, that's just great. Take a look at the result.

ARTEMIS points to the scene below.

ATHENE: So?

ARTEMIS: So that girl Alecto is under my protection and you've got her messed up in your little scheme.

ATHENE: Her? That walking fashion crime in the bearskin?

ARTEMIS: You watch it, you spoiled little brat, or I'll…

ATHENE: Oh, fine. I don't care. I'll give him back his powers. I'm bored with this whole game anyway.

ARTEMIS:	You can't.
ATHENE:	Huh?
ARTEMIS:	You can't give him back his powers.
ATHENE:	What are you talking about?
ARTEMIS:	You can't do a thing for them. Neither can I. They're stuck down there.
ATHENE:	Why?
ARTEMIS:	Because it's the realm of the Graeae.
ATHENE:	The Graeae? Give me a break! Nobody's seen those ugly old biddies in years!
ARTEMIS:	That's because they live in the bowels of the earth, you idiot. They rule down there. The gods of Olympus have no power. If anything happens to my girl, you are going to be one very sorry little…

ATHENE races offstage in a panic, chased by ARTEMIS.

ATHENE:	Papa!

Act II, Scene 2

Underground in the silver mine outside Argenopolis. ALECTO, DIAGORAS, HERMES, ION and PHILEMON are in chains. They work with pickaxes and shovels to the rhythm of a Balkan work song. HERMES and ION speak quietly to one another.

ION:	Why didn't you do something?
HERMES:	I told you. I tried. Nothing happened.
ION:	What was wrong?
HERMES:	I wish I knew. Suddenly it felt like I was shriveling up inside. I promised to keep his son out of trouble and now look. I've got us all into this mess.

PHILEMON struggles to keep up. DIAGORAS works by his side.

ALECTO:	Here. *(tossing a shovelful of rocks into PHILEMON's pile)* That'll keep 'em happy for a while.
DIAGORAS:	Thanks.
ALECTO:	I'm not doing it for you! He's old. He can't keep up. If it weren't for your stupidity he wouldn't be here. None of us would.

ALECTO turns away coldly and continues shoveling. PHILEMON and DIAGORAS move away from her and continue talking quietly.

PHILEMON: She doesn't mean it, son.

DIAGORAS: She's right. This whole mess is my fault.

PHILEMON: Don't torture yourself over it. You haven't told her yet?

DIAGORAS: How can I? She hates me.

PHILEMON: You'll have to do it sometime.

DIAGORAS: I know. I was waiting for the right time.

PHILEMON: I'm not sure there's ever a right time for these things.

ION comes over and works alongside ALECTO.

ION: You know, he didn't mean for this to happen. Why don't you give him a break?

ALECTO: I should never have let myself get sucked in!

ALECTO continues shoveling, furiously.

ION: For someone who hates being a slave you're going at it awfully hard.

ALECTO: Might as well. We're stuck down here. It passes the time.

ION: If you want to fill my pile, go ahead. Be my guest.

ALECTO: *(smiling in spite of herself)* Yeah, right. I tell you what. I'll fill your pile if you'll answer one question for me.

ION: Fire away.

ALECTO: Just who are you, really? You and your friend "Quicksilver"?

ION: I told you. We're slaves.

ALECTO: Yeah, yeah, from a farm outside Thebes. What was your job there?

ION: Job? Oh, I ah… worked the olive press.

ALECTO: Really? Then why are your hands so smooth? They look like you haven't worked a day in your life.

A FOREMAN calls from offstage.

FOREMAN: You! Down there! Shut up and dig.

DIAGORAS: My father's just taking a break.

FOREMAN: No breaks!

DIAGORAS: Look, he's an old man, he's doing his best…

FOREMAN: I said no breaks!

The sound of a whip cracking.

DIAGORAS: I could tear you apart, whip or no whip!

DIAGORAS is restrained by HERMES.

HERMES: Cool it, Diagoras! This is one fight you can't win.

FOREMAN: Hah! Look at the big wrestling champion now! Get back to work, all of you!

ION: *(to HERMES)* How long are we going to have to do this?

HERMES: I don't know.

ION: You think Zeus knows where we are?

HERMES: I have no idea.

ION: Does this mean we're mortal now? Are we just going to stay down here and… Die?

HERMES: Don't you get it? I don't know! I don't know anything anymore!

FOREMAN: *(offstage)* Hey! I told you to stop yammering and get back to work!

The rhythmic monotony of their work continues. A sound of rumbling overhead. They all look up, alarmed.

ION: What's that?

HERMES: I don't know. But I don't like the sound of it.

Another burst of noise, then the sound of falling rock.

ION: You don't suppose…

Shrieks from elsewhere in the mine, followed by a sudden blackout.

HERMES: Get down, Ion!

Act II, Scene 3

Argenopolis, the same day. CLEON's chambers. BAUCIS enters.

BAUCIS: You wanted to see me?

CLEON: You know I want to let that pigheaded husband of yours out of the mine. All he has to do is recant.

BAUCIS: You believe for one second he'd do that?

CLEON:	Talk him into it!
BAUCIS:	I can't.
CLEON:	You know his health can't take it.
BAUCIS:	Release him if you're so worried about his health!
CLEON:	I can't do that! The people need to see that someone's in command.
BAUCIS:	Even if it means taking away the rights of a free citizen?
CLEON:	Everything I've done is within the law.
BAUCIS:	Which you interpret as it suits you.
CLEON:	I do what needs to be done. I don't have the luxury of engaging in the niceties of debate. Oh, Baucis, I wish I could make you understand. I'm not doing this for myself. I am trying with every fiber of my being to build this polis into a force to be reckoned with!
BAUCIS:	There's nothing wrong with your aims, Cleon. But this is the wrong way to go about it. I'm asking you as an old, dear friend. Put politics aside. Act from your heart. Release my husband and son from the mine.
CLEON:	I wish I could, Baucis. But I can't.
BAUCIS:	Then there's nothing more to say.

BAUCIS starts to leave. She notices a shrine in CLEON's chamber and stops suddenly.

CLEON:	What is it?
BAUCIS:	Nothing. *(leaving)*
CLEON:	Baucis, wait. I can't bear to leave things like this between us. We've known one another such a long time. You always were such an independent spirit. Right from when you were a little girl. It's lonely in this job. Since Melanippe died there's no one I can talk to. There was a time when I hoped my parents would choose you for my bride… I know you felt the same way…
BAUCIS:	Cleon, why is there a tablet missing from your shrine to Artemis?
CLEON:	It must have been broken off by a clumsy servant.
BAUCIS:	When?
CLEON:	I don't remember. Why are you so interested?
BAUCIS:	Do you know what happened to it?
CLEON:	The tablet? No.

BAUCIS:	Could the servant have broken it deliberately?
CLEON:	How would I know?
BAUCIS:	Could she have wrapped it in a cloth and put it in a pot at the edge of the agora?
CLEON:	What are you getting at?
BAUCIS:	This.

She hands him the broken tablet pieces, which she has been carrying with her.

CLEON:	What's this?
BAUCIS:	What does it look like?
CLEON:	Two broken pieces of clay. What possible interest do you think I have in…
BAUCIS:	Take them over to the shrine.
CLEON:	No!
BAUCIS:	Then I will. See? They fit perfectly where the tablet has been broken off.
CLEON:	So what if they do?
BAUCIS:	I found one of these pieces in a pot at the edge of the agora, tucked in the swaddling clothes of a newborn baby.
CLEON:	You found it? When?
BAUCIS:	Seventeen years ago, Cleon.
CLEON:	By the gods… Not Diagoras?

BAUCIS nods.

CLEON:	But I always thought… How is that possible?
BAUCIS:	After we found the baby, I went into seclusion. We told everyone the gods had blessed us with a child.
CLEON:	No one had any idea he wasn't yours?
BAUCIS:	No. Not even Diagoras himself. Until a few days ago.
CLEON:	Diagoras. No wonder I always felt… I must have known, somehow, that he was…
BAUCIS:	Why did you have him put out, Cleon?
CLEON:	I already had two sons. My family's fortune was so small. I couldn't

bear the thought of dividing it further. It seemed like the practical thing to do at the time. How could I have known the gods would take both of them from me so young?

BAUCIS: And Melanippe? How did she feel about it?

CLEON: Women are always more soft-hearted about these things.

BAUCIS: So are slaves. The pot was right at the edge of the agora. Whoever left him there knew he'd be found.

CLEON: This changes everything. I won't let Diagoras spend another second in that mine. Baucis, you don't know what this means to me, knowing that I have a son. The gods have given me another chance. I'll have them both released at once.

BAUCIS: Wait.

CLEON: What?

BAUCIS: A son is not all you have.

CLEON: What do you mean?

BAUCIS: Cleon, was the inheritance the only reason you put him out? Or were you worried about something else?

CLEON: What are you getting at?

BAUCIS: About twins bringing shame on your house?

CLEON: *(dumbfounded)* How did you know?

BAUCIS: When I found Diagoras there was only part of the tablet in the pot. The other half... *(holding it up)* ...came from around the neck of the girl, Alecto.

CLEON: That's impossible!

BAUCIS: It's true.

CLEON: There's no way that one could have survived!

BAUCIS: Maybe it's true that she was suckled by a bear. But survive she did. And you did it because of that business about twins being the product of adultery?

CLEON: Of course it's nonsense, but a lot of people take it seriously. I was just starting out in politics. I couldn't afford to get caught up in that kind of scandal.

BAUCIS: You always were concerned about your career.

CLEON: Fine, Baucis. You and Philemon can look down from your pedestal and judge the rest of us. What I did was no different from what countless other fathers have always done. I was fulfilling my duty to my family, doing what was necessary to protect our fortune and good name.

BAUCIS: And your daughter? What about her? Are you going to free her, too?

CLEON: This is all too much. I need time to think!

Commotion offstage.

CLEON: What's going on out there? Wait here, Baucis. I'll be right back.

CLEON exits. Rapid, agitated whispers offstage. CLEON returns.

CLEON: Baucis, something's happened.

BAUCIS: What?

CLEON: There's been a cave-in at the mine.

BAUCIS: A cave-in?

CLEON: Yes.

BAUCIS: How bad?

CLEON: Bad.

BAUCIS tries to run out of the room, screaming.

CLEON: *(trying to restrain her)* Baucis…

They exit.

Act II, Scene 4

Back at the mine, after the cave-in.

ION: Hermes?

HERMES: I'm here.

ION: What happened?

HERMES: The mine's collapsed.

DIAGORAS: Father!

HERMES: Keep still! You could bring it on again!

DIAGORAS: But I have to find my father. Father!

ION: Where's Alecto?

ALECTO: I'm over here.

ION: Are you all right?

DIAGORAS: Where is he? Father!

HERMES: Philemon, are you there?

ION: Philemon!

DIAGORAS: Father!

ALECTO: Quiet!

HERMES: What?

ALECTO: Listen!

A muffled cry.

ALECTO: It's coming from over there!

She tears at the rock with her bare hands. PHILEMON's voice comes through the fallen rock.

PHILEMON: I'm here.

DIAGORAS: Father! Thank the gods!

The others tear away with their pickaxes, finally freeing PHILEMON.

HERMES: He's hurt.

They pull him out, groaning in pain. They try to lift him to a standing position. He collapses.

DIAGORAS: We've got to get him out of here.

ION: How? There's a solid wall of rock.

PHILEMON gasps for breath.

DIAGORAS: What's wrong, father? Is it your leg?

PHILEMON: *(shakes his head)* It's just that I… can't get enough breath.
              The air around us is growing thinner.

HERMES: Thinner? What do you mean?

PHILEMON: There's a substance in the air… We need it to draw breath. You can't
              see it or smell it, but it's there. We're using it up as we breathe and no
              more can get in. You'll all start feeling it soon. We've got to get out of
              here or we'll die.

| ALECTO: | Shhhh! Listen! |

They look at ALECTO who has her ears cocked toward something deeper in the cavern.

ION:	What?
ALECTO:	I hear something.
HERMES:	It could be other survivors.
ALECTO:	Come on.
DIAGORAS:	But that way goes even deeper into the mine. We'll be even more trapped.

Now all of them can hear a faint sound, like the low buzz of distant talking. ALECTO gestures insistently for them to follow her.

ALECTO:	Fine, stay here and die.
HERMES:	Maybe she knows something we don't.
ION:	I'm going with Alecto. If anybody can find a way out of here, it's her.

They enter a passageway, DIAGORAS and ION carrying the limping, weak PHILEMON. The sounds grow louder as they reach a chamber with a higher ceiling deep in the mine. They look up to see an astonishing sight: three giant hags with long gray hair, GRAEA #1, GRAEA #2, and GRAEA #3. Each of their heads has a hole in the center for a single eyeball, which they pass back and forth between them. The hags are in the midst of bickering with one another.

GRAEA #1:	Sister! You've had the eye long enough! Give it to me.
GRAEA #2:	No! It's my turn. I've been waiting longer than you!
GRAEA #3:	No, sister, you always hog it.
GRAEA #1:	Let me keep it a bit longer. I thought I heard something.
GRAEA #2:	What? Falling rock? Big deal!
GRAEA #3:	No, something different, I swear.
GRAEA #1:	I don't hear anything.
GRAEA #2:	Your hearing went a few thousand years ago, sister!
HERMES:	I don't believe this.
GRAEA #3:	See! I told you I heard something!
GRAEA #1:	Give me the eye! I can find it better than you!

She snatches the eye away and peers through it.

GRAEA #2:	Who goes there?
HERMES:	And I thought they were lost in the mists of time!
GRAEA #3:	Who dares defile the sanctuary of the Graeae?
DIAGORAS:	What do we do?
HERMES:	Let me handle this. *(to the GRAEAE)* Our apologies for disturbing you, O Great Gray Sisters. We mean no disrespect.
GRAEA #1:	Then get out of here!
GRAEA #2:	Beat it!
HERMES:	We wish we could. We're trapped down here. The mine's collapsed.
GRAEA #3:	Of course it has!
GRAEA #1:	You stupid mortal!
GRAEA #2:	We made it happen!

Laughter among the GRAEAE.

ION:	You? Why?
GRAEA #3:	To stop your infernal hacking and pounding!
GRAEA #1:	How are we supposed to get any sleep with all that racket, day and night?
GRAEA #2:	Sister, you wouldn't know daytime if it came up and bit you on the ass!
GRAEA #3:	Shut up!
DIAGORAS:	But there were hundreds of slaves working down here!
GRAEA #1:	Yes. And they're under piles of rock now!
GRAEA #2:	Flat as pancakes!

More laughter from the GRAEAE.

ION:	How could you do that?
GRAEA #3:	Oh boo-hoo!
GRAEA #1:	We're just old hags. We can do what we want.
GRAEA #2:	Come on, sister, time to ante up the eye. I haven't had a look yet!
GRAEA #3:	*(passing the eye)* You'll be disappointed. They're a pathetic lot! Except the young hunk there.

GRAEA #2: *(taking the eye, looking through it)* Oh, he's cute. Look at those muscles!

HERMES: Gray Ones, you know this cave. Just tell us a way out and we'll go…

GRAEA #2: *(peering down at HERMES)* You, come closer. You look strangely familiar.

HERMES: I do?

GRAEA #2: Like some god I met once.

GRAEA #3: What? One of those slimebags from Olympus? *(grabbing the eye to have a look)* Nope. Too puny.

GRAEA #1: Doesn't smell bad enough either!

The GRAEAE laugh uproariously at their own joke.

ION: Where do you get off mocking the gods of Olympus?

GRAEA #1: *(mocking tone)* "Where do you get off blah blah blah…"

GRAEA #2: What are you, some sucky little brown-noser priest?

PHILEMON is gasping for breath.

DIAGORAS: My father's hurt. He can hardly breathe. We've got to get him out of here or he'll die!

GRAEA #3: You all will!

GRAEA #1: A few less mortals to bother us.

GRAEA #2: The Graeae care nothing for human life!

ALECTO: Neither do I!

GRAEA #2: Oh, get a load of that one, sister. *(passing the eye)*

ALECTO: I'm not like them.

GRAEA #3: Yes, there's something about her. She's different from the other mortals…

DIAGORAS: Alecto, what are you doing?

ALECTO: It's true. I'm not human! Come closer and I'll show you.

The GRAEAE all bend down, trying to peer through the eye at once.

ALECTO: That's it… Closer…

One of the GRAEAE leans directly over ALECTO and peers at her through the eye. ALECTO suddenly reaches up and snatches the eye away.

GRAEA #1: Ahhhh!

GRAEA #2:	What is it, sister?
GRAEA #3:	What's going on?
GRAEA #1:	She took our eye! I can't see!
GRAEA #2:	You sniveling creature!
GRAEA #3:	Give it back!
ALECTO:	No! Not until you tell us the way out of here!
GRAEA #2:	There is no way out!
ALECTO:	There's got to be!

The GRAEAE wail.

GRAEA #1:	Give it back!
GRAEA #2:	It's no use to you.
GRAEA #3:	There's no way out.
ALECTO:	Then make one! You brought that rockslide on. You can make a passageway out of here.
GRAEA #1:	Are we going to let ourselves be ordered around by a mortal?
GRAEA #2:	I can't stand this darkness.
ALECTO:	Then get us out of here! Do it!

A great, reluctant groaning from the GRAEAE, followed by a rumbling sound. A shaft of light reveals the opening of a passageway.

GRAEA #3:	There!
GRAEA #1:	Are you satisfied?
GRAEA #2:	Give it back!
ALECTO:	Not so fast. How do I know you won't make another collapse before we get out?
GRAEA #3:	We won't.
ALECTO:	Swear!
GRAEA #1:	We promise.
ALECTO:	Swear that if you do you'll be cursed to live in eternal darkness!
GRAEA #2:	But…
ALECTO:	Say it!

GRAEA #2:	I swear if I make the mine collapse…
ALECTO:	All of you!
GRAEAE:	*(mumbling in reluctant unison)* May I be cursed to live in eternal darkness.
ALECTO:	Good. Here!

ALECTO hands over the eye. The GRAEAE take it and exit, screeching.

GRAEA #3:	Oh, the shame!
GRAEA #1:	Tricked by a mortal!
GRAEA #2:	You were stupid to let her get the eye!
GRAEA #3:	Me! It was you who knuckled under to that curse!
GRAEA #1:	You're both idiots!

The GRAEAE exit.

ALECTO:	Let's get moving.
PHILEMON:	You go on.
DIAGORAS:	Father, the way's clear now. Come on, we'll carry you.
PHILEMON:	Wait. There's something I need to say.
DIAGORAS:	Save your breath till we get out of here…
PHILEMON:	No! I want to speak now.

The sound of rumbling from deep in the mine.

PHILEMON:	Diagoras, you can't let Cleon destroy everything your mother and I have worked for. You have to go back and finish your training for the Olympiad.
DIAGORAS:	That's not important now…
PHILEMON:	It is! With the olive crown you'll have influence that I never had. The people will listen to you…
DIAGORAS:	I don't care about the people. I hate them for what they've done to you!
PHILEMON:	You have to promise me.
DIAGORAS:	Father, please…
PHILEMON:	Promise!
DIAGORAS:	Okay, I promise. Now let us get you out of here.

PHILEMON:	No.
DIAGORAS:	What?
PHILEMON:	Go on without me.
DIAGORAS:	I'm not going to leave you here!
PHILEMON:	You have to. I'm slowing you all down. There isn't time.

More rumblings.

HERMES:	He's right. The mine's unstable. We've got to get out of here soon.
ION:	But the Graeae swore they wouldn't make any more trouble!
HERMES:	I'm not sure it's the Graeae doing this.
DIAGORAS:	Father, please…
PHILEMON:	Do as I say! Tell your mother I love her.
DIAGORAS:	Father!

DIAGORAS clings to PHILEMON. HERMES, ALECTO and ION pull him away. As they start through the passageway, HERMES pauses.

HERMES:	*(to ION)* Go on. I'll just be a minute.

The others exit through the passageway. HERMES kneels down next to PHILEMON.

PHILEMON:	Go on, Quicksilver. Don't be a fool.
HERMES:	My name's not Quicksilver. And if I had my staff I'd show you who I am. But I have nothing.
PHILEMON:	Hermes! I should have realized it was you. But how?
HERMES:	Something happened to me. I don't understand what. It's sure given me a taste of mortality, but the funny thing is, I wouldn't trade the experience for anything. Except for the fact that I've let you down so badly. You're dying and I can't do a thing to save you.
PHILEMON:	Don't do this to yourself, my friend. None of us ever knows what the Fates are going to throw at us. Now, go. The ferryman is coming for me. I can feel he's not far away. I'm ready.

PHILEMON lies down and closes his eyes.

HERMES:	Farewell, Philemon. I knew about the weakness of gods but you taught me about the greatness of mortals.

He covers PHILEMON's body and exits.

Act II, Scene 5

ION, ALECTO, DIAGORAS and HERMES emerge from the mine into the daylight, gasping for breath. DIAGORAS is distraught, waves the others away.

ION: *(to HERMES)* I can't believe Zeus would do this to us. Athene must've really worked on him.

HERMES: I don't think it was Zeus.

ION: But you said it wasn't the Graeae either.

HERMES: No, they talk like they have the power to move the earth, but they don't really.

ION: Then who was it?

HERMES: I don't know, little brother. Maybe there's something else.

ION: Something else?

HERMES: Something more powerful than the gods.

ION: What could be more powerful than Zeus?

HERMES: Ion, these past few days have made me realize just how much I don't understand. Like Philemon, talking about that substance in the air you can't see or smell. Even the gods don't know about these things. There must be way more to this life than we can begin to understand.

ION: You are weirding me out, man.

ALECTO approaches them.

ALECTO: Sorry to interrupt…

ION: No, no, it's okay.

ALECTO: I just wanted to say goodbye.

ION: Where are you going?

ALECTO: Back where I came from. You're heading back to Thebes, I suppose?

ION and HERMES nod sheepishly.

HERMES: Yeah.

ION: But we're in no hurry.

ALECTO: Thought you had family there.

ION: Alecto, we're not really from Thebes. And we're not slaves.

ALECTO:	I know. Then who are you?
ION:	It's… complicated.
ALECTO:	It's okay. You don't have to explain. I guess I'll be on my way.

DIAGORAS notices ALECTO preparing to leave.

DIAGORAS:	What? You're leaving?
ALECTO:	Yes.
DIAGORAS:	You're not coming back to Argenopolis with me?
ALECTO:	Why? What good would it do now?
DIAGORAS:	We can't just let Cleon get away with everything he's done.
ALECTO:	It's not my fight.
DIAGORAS:	What about Zoe? Don't you even care what happens to her?
ALECTO:	Yes, but there's nothing I can do for her.
DIAGORAS:	There is! You heard my father. I made a promise to him. Please come back with me. We need each other.
ALECTO:	I don't need anybody.

ALECTO starts to leave.

DIAGORAS:	Alecto! The tablet you wore around your neck!
ALECTO:	What about it?
DIAGORAS:	My mother has it.
ALECTO:	How did she get it?
DIAGORAS:	It caught on my clothes when we fought in the agora. My mother has another piece of the same tablet. It was tied around my wrist when she found me in the agora. When I was a baby.
ALECTO:	You were put out in the agora?
DIAGORAS:	Yes.
ALECTO:	Why are you telling me this?
DIAGORAS:	Alecto, the two pieces fit together perfectly. They formed Artemis' bow. They came from the same place.
ALECTO:	I don't know what you're talking about.
DIAGORAS:	Yes, you do. Just put two and two together.

ALECTO:	This is crazy.
DIAGORAS:	Look at us.
ION:	Whoa!
HERMES:	I can't believe I missed it.
DIAGORAS:	You're my sister.
ALECTO:	I'm nobody's sister!

ALECTO starts to run off.

ION:	Alecto, wait!
ALECTO:	Leave me alone! All of you!

ALECTO exits. ION follows after her.

HERMES:	Ion?
ION:	Hermes, I have to tell you something… I'm not going back to Olympus.
HERMES:	Are you serious?
ION:	Yeah.
HERMES:	You're going to stay? Become mortal?
ION:	Uh-huh.
HERMES:	You know what this means, don't you? There's no going back.
ION:	I know. Am I crazy to do this?
HERMES:	No, you're not.

HERMES and ION embrace.

HERMES:	Now, go on. Catch up with her.

ION exits.

DIAGORAS:	I don't understand her at all. Why turn away from your flesh and blood?
HERMES:	Families can be a frustrating business. Believe me, I know. I'm so sorry about your father, Diagoras. He was a good man.
DIAGORAS:	If I hadn't been so stupid he'd still be alive.
HERMES:	Don't blame yourself. We've all done things we can't change. What will you do now?

DIAGORAS:	I have to go back and break the news to my mother.
HERMES:	I'll walk back with you.
DIAGORAS:	You don't have to do that, Quicksilver. What if the hoplites catch you again?
HERMES:	Don't worry, they won't.

They exit.

Act II, Scene 6

ALECTO stops running, out of breath. ARTEMIS watches her, unseen. ION enters.

ALECTO:	I said leave me alone.
ION:	You're not getting rid of me that easy.
ALECTO:	I'm not going back.
ION:	Okay, then. I'll stay here with you.
ALECTO:	Out here? In the middle of nowhere? What's with you?
ION:	I'm just like you. I'm leaving behind everything I've ever known. Look, you can turn your back on the rest of them if you want. But please, not me. I want to share my life with you, Alecto.

ION extends his hand toward ALECTO. HERMES enters, also unseen except by ARTEMIS, and watches as ALECTO stands silently looking at ION's outstretched hand.

ARTEMIS:	Oh, little one. I've watched over you since the day they left you on that mountainside. But I can't keep you under my wing forever. Fly away, little bird. I release you.

ALECTO extends her hand and grasps ION's. They exit together.

HERMES:	There they go, sister.
ARTEMIS:	Yes, brother. They're on their own now.
HERMES:	It's hard to let them go.
ARTEMIS:	I hear you've had a bit of an adventure lately. Courtesy of our dear baby sister.
HERMES:	Athene! Why am I not surprised? Just wait'll I get my hands around that sweet little neck.
ARTEMIS:	So it's back to Olympus, then?

HERMES:	Where else? I am the messenger boy, after all.
ARTEMIS:	You're also the one who never gives up trying to get them to do the right thing.
HERMES:	It's what I do. Don't suppose you'd care to join me?
ARTEMIS:	Not a chance, brother. I washed my hands of that messed-up bunch eons ago.

HERMES and ARTEMIS exit.

Act II, Scene 7

The outskirts of Argenopolis. DIAGORAS, walking alone. ION and ALECTO enter.

DIAGORAS:	What are you doing here?
ALECTO:	I changed my mind. I want to set things right. But we'll do things my way, understand?
DIAGORAS:	What do you mean?
ALECTO:	Cleon's responsible for the death of Philemon and all those slaves. He has to be brought to justice.
DIAGORAS:	Yeah. And I promised my father I'd try to make the assembly see what he's done.
ALECTO:	Forget the stupid assembly! Don't you see it's useless? He controls everything. A man like Cleon only understands one kind of power. I say we give him a taste of his own medicine.

ALECTO takes out her knife.

DIAGORAS:	What are you saying?
ALECTO:	We'll go to Cleon's. You go in, Ion and I will hang back, out of sight.
DIAGORAS:	He'll just have me arrested.
ALECTO:	No he won't. You're his little trophy! He'll be so glad to see you're alive after that cave-in he'll embrace you with open arms. And then…

Alecto hands him the knife. They look at one another a moment. Suddenly ALECTO takes back the knife and makes a slash on her own arm.

| DIAGORAS: | What are you doing? Are you insane? |
| ALECTO: | We're going to follow the way of my namesake, the Furies. Put out your arm. |

DIAGORAS wordlessly holds out his arm. ALECTO slashes it. They touch their bloodied arms together.

ALECTO: Blood of my blood.

DIAGORAS: Blood of my blood.

ALECTO: Death to Cleon.

DIAGORAS: Death to Cleon.

ION: Whoa.

ALECTO, DIAGORAS and ION exit.

Act II, Scene 8

CLEON's chambers. CLEON and BAUCIS are just finishing a ritual offering to Hades. BAUCIS weeps softly, comforted by CLEON.

CLEON: I'm so sorry, Baucis. It's terrible, what the gods ask of us sometimes.

DIAGORAS enters.

DIAGORAS: Mother!

CLEON: Diagoras!

BAUCIS: *(embracing DIAGORAS)* Thank the gods! I thought you were dead.

DIAGORAS: I tried to save father, but I couldn't…

BAUCIS: I know.

DIAGORAS: He told me to tell you he loved you.

BAUCIS: Oh, my boy…

CLEON: Diagoras, I'm so sorry. Philemon's death is a terrible tragedy. But there's something we have to tell you. Argenopolis has lost a great citizen, but you still have a father.

DIAGORAS: What are you talking about?

CLEON: The mystery of your birth has been solved. The woman who gave birth to you was my late wife, Melanippe.

DIAGORAS: What?

BAUCIS: It's true, Diagoras.

DIAGORAS: Are you sure?

BAUCIS:	There. The broken shrine to Artemis? The pieces of the tablet fit it perfectly.
DIAGORAS:	So it's you? You're the one who had me put out?
CLEON:	Yes, it was a terrible thing to do. It's the greatest regret of my life, Diagoras. But to discover that I have a son, and that it's you, the young man I regard more highly than anyone in the polis. I want to make up for lost time. I want to acknowledge you as my son.
DIAGORAS:	You want me to call you father?
CLEON:	Yes. I'd be honored.
DIAGORAS:	I have a father, Cleon. His name is Philemon.
CLEON:	I know how strongly you must feel toward the man who raised you…
BAUCIS:	How dare you claim the son Philemon and I raised as your own? You ordered him put out! You sent them down into the mine!
CLEON:	You're overwhelmed by grief, Baucis. You don't know what you're saying.
DIAGORAS:	She knows exactly what she's saying! I've lost my father because of you.
CLEON:	You can't blame me for the cave-in! The gods caused it, not me.
DIAGORAS:	You knew he wasn't fit to go down there. He was old and frail and that's why he couldn't make it out.
CLEON:	Diagoras, I was just about to have you both released when I got word of the cave-in. I swear it! You can ask Baucis!
DIAGORAS:	Is that true?
BAUCIS:	Yes. Everything changed as soon as he learned you were his son.
CLEON:	You both have every right to be angry with me. I can only pray the gods you can find it in your heart to forgive me. Please, Diagoras. Let's try to put the past behind us. I want you at my side. I want us to work together to rebuild Argenopolis and help her achieve her glorious destiny.

ALECTO and ION enter. ALECTO races toward CLEON, pounces on him and holds a knife to his throat.

ALECTO:	*(challenging DIAGORAS)* Go on! What are you waiting for? Do it!
DIAGORAS:	I can't.
ALECTO:	Then I will.

DIAGORAS:	No, Alecto! Wait! You can't do this. He's our father.
ALECTO:	That's not true!
DIAGORAS:	Yes, it is!
BAUCIS:	Here. See for yourself! *(showing her the tablet pieces)*
CLEON:	You don't dare murder your own father.
ALECTO:	Family doesn't mean a thing to me!
CLEON:	No? Remember the curse of Oedipus!
ION:	Hold on, Alecto. You might want to rethink this one.
ALECTO:	I don't care about your curses. I'm not bound by your laws.

ALECTO is poised to drive the knife into CLEON. DIAGORAS restrains her.

DIAGORAS:	Alecto! Don't do this. No one has the right to take another life.
ALECTO:	We made an oath in blood!
DIAGORAS:	I got carried away. I didn't know what I was doing! Please, Alecto. No more killing.
BAUCIS:	If it's justice you want, Alecto, there's another punishment. One that's just as severe.
ALECTO:	What?
BAUCIS:	By casting the ostraka, the assembly has the power to ban a person from the polis for life.
ALECTO:	So? Why should he be allowed to live?
BAUCIS:	He'll be stripped of his home, his ancestry, everything that makes his life worth living.
DIAGORAS:	It's almost worse than dying.
ALECTO:	Even if that's true, your assembly's nothing but words and lies.
DIAGORAS:	That's not what my father believed, Alecto. You heard the promise I made to him. Philemon believed that human beings have the power to rise above vengeance and hatred. He always said we have to find a new way of working together and that way was democracy. Please give it a chance, Alecto. Let the people decide what happens to Cleon.

ALECTO considers, and then finally hands DIAGORAS the knife.

ALECTO:	Here. The people better be right.

CLEON: They certainly won't be foolish enough to banish the leader who's brought them prosperity. *(to ALECTO)* And if you're lucky, they'll let you go back to living like the animal you are.

DIAGORAS: We'll see.

All exit.

Act II, Scene 9

Ritual music. DIAGORAS and CLEON enter and face the assembly. Behind them, BAUCIS, ALECTO and ION enter, carrying pottery jugs. In sequence, each one pours out the broken pottery shards (ostraka). Black for yes, white for no. The vote is for banishment.

DIAGORAS: From this day onward, Cleon is banished from Argenopolis, the place of his birth, for as long as he shall live.

CLEON is stripped of his magistrate's robes by BAUCIS. CLEON exits. The music changes to celebratory. DIAGORAS, BAUCIS, ALECTO, ION join in a circle dance. ATHENE enters, notices the festivities.

ATHENE: All right! A party!

ATHENE races down to join the circle dance. The others look mystified, don't recognize her, but let her join in. HERMES enters and catches sight of ATHENE. ATHENE sees him, breaks out of the circle, screaming. HERMES chases after her.

ATHENE: Papa!!!!

THE END

GLOSSARY OF THEATER TERMS

ACT Divisions between major segments of a play. Acts can be further divided into scenes. Most modern plays have one or two acts, but in Shakespeare's day, there could be dozens.

ACTORS Individuals who, usually under contract, portray characters and roles in the play. The term "actor" applies to males and females.

AD LIB To improvise words and actions; spontaneous acting without a script.

ANTAGONIST The opposite of PROTAGONIST in a play; the villain.

ASIDE A line spoken by an actor to the audience, and that is not supposed to be heard by the other actors on the stage.

AUDITION Competitive try-out for a performer seeking a role in a theater production. The actor always brings her or his résumé and headshot to the audition. The process may include interviews, the reciting of a prepared piece (usually a MONOLOGUE or block of dialogue spoken by one character from a play), readings from the script of the play being auditioned for, or any combination of these. Sometimes several actors audition together, reading a scene with several roles.

BACKDROP A large sheet of painted canvas or muslin, or a "flat" that hangs or sits at the back wall of the stage set.

BACKSTAGE The part of the stage that is out of sight of the audience, including the service areas of the theater and the dressing rooms.

BIT PART A small role with little dialogue.

BLACKOUT A fast darkening of the stage; when the stage lights are all turned off.

BLACK-BOX THEATER Very plain, flexible space used for theater performances, and generally painted black (hence the term) so that it can be modified easily to allow the imagination of the audience to visualize the scenery. In this type of space the audience seating and acting areas can be arranged in any way that suits the individual needs of the specific production.

BLOCKING The process by which the director arranges the action and movement of the actors during the play. This helps with other aspects of the production, like where to place props and furniture, because the movement of the actors is predictable and regular.

BOX OFFICE The place where tickets are sold for admission to performances.

BREAK A LEG! The traditional way that theater people wish one another good luck; the term "good luck" is considered bad luck, and saying "break a leg!" rose out of that superstition.

CALL Announcement to actors and crew that they are needed for a rehearsal or performance; a warning to actors to be prepared for their entrance. Calls are normally made by the STAGE MANAGER.

CAST The members of the acting company.

CASTING The process of choosing actors to perform roles in the play. Usually conducted by the director, often with input from the playwright and producer.

CATHARSIS When a moment of high tragedy at the emotional CLIMAX of the play is followed by resolution and conclusion.

CATWALKS Narrow platforms suspended above the stage to permit ready access to the ropes, lights and scenery that are hung from the "grid."

CENTER STAGE (CS) The middle portion of the stage floor. This area affords good sightlines from all seats in the theater.

CHEWING THE SCENERY An actor who gives a hammed-up, over-the-top performance is said to be "chewing the scenery."

CHOREOGRAPHER The member of the production's creative team who sets movement sequences and designs dance movements for the play or musical. Also used in ballet.

CHORUS Popular in ancient Greek theater, this continues to be a mainstay technique in modern plays. The chorus is a character or group that comments on the action, and thereby advances the plot, somewhat like a cheering section. Often created by use of a crowd, but sometimes not actually seen on the stage; just heard from OFFSTAGE. In the case of a musical, the chorus comprises the singers and/or dancers in large ENSEMBLE numbers.

CLIMAX Highest point of dramatic tension in a play when the major conflict can go no further without triggering the ending of the play.

CLOSING The last night of a play's performance RUN.

COLLECTIVE CREATION / COLLABORATIVE A play created by a group, rather than being written by a single playwright. Usually a group of actors who base the story and characters on their collected ideas.

COMEDY A play with humor that ends happily.

COMIC RELIEF Inclusion of a comic line or scene to inject a light moment into an otherwise serious play.

COMMEDIA DELL'ARTE A form of comedy based in the Italian Renaissance, but that endures in modern theater. Using a group of stock characters like Harlequin, Captain, Doctor, Pantaloon, Pulcinella, etc., each identified by masks, the performances are based on each character's "lazzi," or business, and are largely improvised.

COMP The short form of "complimentary ticket." Free tickets issued to special guests or company members; each theater company has its own policy regarding the number of comps issued and to whom.

COMPANY The PRODUCER, PLAYWRIGHT, DRAMATURG, DIRECTORS, STAGE MANAGERS, DESIGNERS, COMPOSER, CAST and STAGE CREW associated with a specific theater production.

COMPOSER The person engaged to write the score, incidental music, music for song lyrics, and scene "bumpers" (short segments of music, usually a couple of bars, that segue or transition one scene into the next). This person sometimes also assumes the role of MUSIC DIRECTOR. The composer writes music and is usually capable of playing a range of musical instruments.

CONDUCTOR The director of an orchestra. See also MUSICAL DIRECTOR.

CONTROL BOOTH The light/projection and sound booth generally located at the rear of the auditorium. It houses lighting and sound equipment, and it is often from the booth that the STAGE MANAGER runs the show.

COSTUME DESIGNER (see also DESIGNER) The person assigned to design the costumes for the play; he or she does research on the historical period of the play, and designs the costumes based on the research and who is cast in each role in the play. Also does detailed drawings of the costumes (often in full-color), selects fabrics and accessories, works with the "cutter," the person who drafts the costume patterns and cuts the fabric, to ensure the designs are adhered to, and then participates in fitting the costumes on the actors.

CUE Signal in the form of a line of dialogue or specific action to an actor or stage technician that indicates the next action or dialogue is to occur.

CUT-TO-CUE A technical rehearsal in which the action and dialogue are cut out. This enables the technical crew, including sound and light operators, to plot their activities according to the timing of each CUE.

CURTAIN CALL At the end of a performance, when the actors acknowledge audience applause.

CURTAIN TIME The publicly stated starting time of the performance.

DARK A day when there is no production staged at the theater, often the only day off for the cast and crew.

DESIGNER Also called "Theater Designer," this is the person who designs both sets and costumes, effectively creating a trademark look and feel for the entire production. The designer is responsible for the images seen on stage, from the largest backdrop, to the earrings the actors might wear, to the style of hair and the amount of make-up. The picture the designer creates is a lasting image the audience won't soon forget.

DEUS EX MACHINA Originally a theatrical device in ancient Greek and Roman theaters where a god would appear above the scenery at the end of a play and resolve all the conflicts. It has evolved to become the term used to describe any event happening late in the play that — somewhat miraculously — provides a resolution to the conflict.

DIALECT COACH Specialist who is brought in to train actors in the delivery of a specific accent or dialect.

DIALOGUE The spoken text of a play. Conversation between characters is dialogue.

DIRECTOR In modern theater, the person who interprets and brings to the stage the playwright's script. The director must provide artistic meaning to the script, infusing it with the proper emphasis, imagery and thematic consistency. In musicals, the musical director and choreographer work closely with the director.

DOUBLE TAKE When an actor looks at something or someone, looks away, then realizes what it actually was she or he has seen or heard, and quickly looks back.

DOUBLING When a single actor handles several roles in one play. For example, a play might have nine roles, but all those can be handled by, say, three actors.

DOWNSTAGE (DS) The part of the stage nearest to the audience. There are also downstage right (DSR) and downstage left (DSL). The opposite of UPSTAGE.

DRAMA A serious form of theater that takes a thoughtful, sober attitude toward its subject matter.

DRAMATIST A playwright.

DRAMATURG Either an individual who free-lances doing dramaturgy for playwrights, or a member of a theater company who acts as a script consultant and editor. The dramaturg generally works with new scripts and helps develop them so that the transition from paper to stage production is smooth, accurate and practical. In some cases, when a producer or playwright wants a script changed or reduced, a dramaturg is brought in to help with that process; the thinking is that the playwright might be too close to his or her own script to handle an objective set of changes to the script.

DRESS REHEARSAL A full rehearsal, sometimes with an invited audience, with all technical and artistic elements brought together, including costumes. It strives to duplicate, as far as possible, an actual performance of the play, but can be stopped and adjusted by the director.

DRESSER The person who assists actors with their costumes before, during and after a performance.

DRESSING ROOM A space where performers change into and out of their costumes, put on make-up, and otherwise prepare for the show.

ENSEMBLE An acting group, normally where one actor does not outshine the others.

ENTRANCE Either the moment when an actor enters the stage area, or an opening in the set for actors to pass through when entering the stage area.

ENVIRONMENTAL THEATER An experimental, largely contemporary concept of mixing the audience and the actors in a flexible space where the action occurs all around the room. In some environmental theater, the audience actually sits on the stage.

EPILOGUE Speech or short scene that sometimes follows the main action of a play, and tells or shows what occurred after the main part of the play ended.

EXIT The moment when an actor leaves the stage area.

EXPOSITION Places in the script where the playwright supplies the background information necessary for a complete understanding of the play.

EXTRA An actor who is on stage to provide atmosphere (as in a crowd scene), but only speaks as part of a group and has no individual lines.

FADE OUT / DIM OUT A slow darkening of the stage lights.

FADE UP / FADE IN When the stage lights come up gradually.

FARCE Comic play where humor is primarily physical. Farce relies less on dialogue than do the so-called "higher forms" of comedy.

FLASHBACK Theatrical (and literary) technique in which scenes from the past are acted in the present moment; still, it is clear that they are in the past.

FOG MACHINE A machine that produces ground-hugging fog by melting dry ice.

FOOTLIGHTS Lights placed in a row along the front (downstage) of a stage floor.

FORESHADOWING Dialogue in one part of a play that hints at something that will happen later in the production.

FREEZE The stopping of all movement in the play.

FRONT-OF-HOUSE (FOH) The part of the theater that is in front of the stage, including the audience seating, foyer or lobby, box office, etc. The back-stage areas are known as REAR-OF-HOUSE (ROH).

GENRE The type of play, or style of performance. For example, comedy, tragedy, farce, pantomime, history.

GREEN ROOM Traditional name of the room in which actors wait for their entrances. The name came from London's Drury Lane Theatre, where that room was actually colored green; green rooms in modern theaters are painted a range of colors and are "green" in name only.

HAM A person who engages in exaggerated over-acting.

HEAVY (THE) A villain.

HOUSE Rows of seats in which the audience sits to watch a performance; also a basic reference to a building that "houses" a theater.

HOUSE LIGHTS Lights that illuminate the auditorium portion of a theater; all the lights in the auditorium except the "exit" sign lights. These lights are usually dimmed during a performance and are controlled from the CONTROL BOOTH.

IMPROVISATION / IMPROV Type of performing in which actors work without a script, inventing the dialogue and action as they perform.

IN-THE-ROUND A form of seating layout where the acting area is enclosed on virtually all sides by the audience. There are normally a number of entranceways inserted throughout the seating. In this set-up, the placement of objects on the stage must be carefully done so as not to obscure the audience's view.

INTERMISSION / INTERVAL Break between sections or ACTS of a performance. During a play the intermission is normally roughly half way through a full-length (or two-act) play with approximately 60 to 90 minutes per act. The intermission is usually 15 or 20 minutes long.

LIBRETTO Text of an opera or musical. Also known as "the book."

LIGHTING DESIGNER Works closely with the technical director and DESIGNER. Responsible for the overall look of the lighting; the person who decides where lights should go, how they should be positioned and colored, and which ones should be on at any given time.

LYRICIST Author of the words of a song.

MASK A device that disguises the face of the wearer and/or identifies the stage character of the wearer.

MASQUE A form of theater where the actors cover their faces with masks. Common images used in masques are images from nature, like the sun, the moon and the stars.

MATINEE Afternoon performance of a show; the normal matinee CURTAIN TIME is two o'clock.

MELODRAMA Suspenseful, plot-oriented drama featuring all-good heroes and all-bad villains.

MEZZANINE Lower section of the second tier of audience seating in a theater.

MIME Form of performance with no spoken words; also the performer who does this type of show. The story and characters are conveyed to the audience by movement and gesture, especially animated facial expressions.

MONOLOGUE A speech in a play delivered by a single actor who is often alone on the stage. See also SOLILOQUY.

MOTIF Recurring theme or a pattern of repetition in the elements of a production. Also integral to visual art and interior design.

MUGGING Use of excessive, exaggerated expressions.

MUSICAL DIRECTOR The person responsible for the musical content of a production, be it an actual musical, or a non-musical play with musical effects.

OFF-BOOK When an actor can perform his or her lines from memory.

OFFSTAGE Areas of the stage not in view of the audience.

ONE-ACT PLAY Generally, a shorter play consisting of one act and no intermission.

ONE-HANDER A play where there is only one actor, even if the actor plays several roles. Similarly, a two-hander is for two actors, and so on.

OPENING The first official public performance of a play.

OPERA Highly dramatic (although there are comic operas) and stylized form of theater in which the dialogue is almost completely sung.

ORCHESTRA Main floor seating of the auditorium; also a group of musicians that play the songs in musicals and in OPERAS.

ORCHESTRA PIT The area housing the conductor and musicians. This was originally a lower "pit" section between the front of the stage and the first row of audience seats, but it is now more loosely used to describe any area around the stage where the conductor and musicians perform.

OVERTURE Orchestral beginning of a musical, opera or play; usually a summary of all the songs or score of the show.

PACING The timing of lines and action as they are performed. Good pacing ensures that there are no lingering gaps where there shouldn't be and that dialogue does not overlap, unless it is meant to for dramatic effect. Proper pacing is essential to comedy.

PAPER THE HOUSE Marketing technique of giving away tickets to a performance to make a show seem to be selling better than it actually is, and by so doing, hoping that word-of-mouth advertising sells tickets.

PLAYING SPACE The available area of the stage that can be used for the performance. This does not include any part of the stage that is not visible to the audience.

PLAYWRIGHT The writer of the script for a play. The playwright may adapt existing stories to be performed on a stage, or write original plays from her or his own ideas. This is the first, and often most creative, artist of those who will collaborate on a theater production. It is the playwright's script that serves as the template for the full production. In the case of musicals, the person or people who write the book, music, and lyrics are considered to be the writers.

PRESET The placement of sets, furniture and props put in position at the beginning of a scene or act. This is what the audience will see when it enters the auditorium (unless a curtain is used to hide the stage).

PREVIEW Performance or performances staged before the play officially opens, and aimed at helping the director judge audience reaction. Sometimes audience members are invited to previews, or preview tickets will be sold at reduced prices. By this point in the production, the play should be performance-ready, but the preview gives the director one last chance, with audience reaction, to make adjustments before OPENING night.

PRODUCER The person or organization responsible for the organizational, financial and contractual side of a production. His or her duties can also include raising money, renting facilities, employing the director, designers, composer, technical crew, front-of-house staff, marketing and public relations people, and, in conjunction with the director, the cast. The producer works closely with the creative team (director, designers, composer) before embarking on a production, and often selects the play or plays to be produced (sometimes done in conjunction with an artistic director, if it is a large production company).

PRODUCTION NUMBER Large showtune with lots of singers, dancers, spectacular scenery, beautiful costumes, and glittering lighting.

PROJECTION Actors' technique for making his or her voice travel clearly to all parts of the HOUSE. This term can also be used to describe an extension of the apron at the front of the stage; also a BACKDROP created with the use of cameras, projectors or other electronic equipment.

PROLOGUE A speech or a short scene preceding the main body of the play that helps set the mood and often gives background information for the story.

PROMPTER Person who holds the "prompt book" (a complete copy of the script) offstage during rehearsals and performances, and provides lead-in lines to performers who have forgotten all or part of their dialogue.

PROPS / PROPERTIES These include furnishings, set dressings, decorations, and all items, large and small that are not classified as scenery, electrics or wardrobe. Props used by actors are known as hand props (an example would be a cane); props which are kept in an actor's costume are called personal props (for example, a handkerchief tucked in a pocket).

PROSCENIUM ARCH There are several types of theater stages and one of these is the proscenium arch (see also THRUST STAGE). This type looks like a picture frame around a stage that is set back from the frame. The stage sometimes protrudes past the frame, and that part is called the apron. It is nicknamed "the fourth wall" and often shortened to just "proscenium" or "pros arch." In some older theaters the proscenium arch is ornate and painted to contrast with the adjacent walls. Except for the stage apron, it is tradition that nothing outside the proscenium arch is part of the play. Other types of theater stages include IN-THE-ROUND, and Studio; the latter often has no fixed stage at all and involves flexible space.

PROTAGONIST The leading character or hero in a play; the one who opposes the ANTAGONIST.

PUBLIC DOMAIN Any work of literature, including plays, musicals, operas, and songs, that is not under copyright and can be used by the PRODUCER or PLAYWRIGHT without the payment of ROYALTIES to the original creator of the piece. In most countries a property becomes public domain 75 years after the author's death.

PUBLICITY The department of the production company that deals with selling tickets to the play or plays being produced; also involving marketing, advertising, and public relations.

PUNCHLINE The line of dialogue that concludes a joke and should get a laugh.

READ-THROUGH Usually the first rehearsal is a read-through; the cast reads through the play together, often stopping to ask questions regarding character development, dialogue, pronunciation and action.

REAR-OF-HOUSE (ROH) The BACKSTAGE and storage areas of the theater. See also FRONT-OF-HOUSE (FOH).

RECITATIVE Operatic dialogue sung in a style that suggests the inflections of speech; more like sung words than a song, per se.

REFRAIN Main part of a song, often having thirty-two measures.

REHEARSAL The period of work and pre-production preparation that mostly involves the director and actors. Rehearsals include a READ-

THROUGH, BLOCKING, and repeated practicing of the roles, both dialogue and action. Later in the process, there are technical rehearsals and a DRESS REHEARSAL.

REPERTORY THEATER A theater company that produces more than one play in a season, and runs two or more plays, perhaps some of them simultaneously in different theaters.

REPRISE In musicals, the repetition of a song or dance, often with some variations.

REVIEW A THEATER CRITIC's written assessment of his or her opinion of a play.

REVUE A type of performance consisting of light-hearted songs and comic sketches — a variety show or cabaret.

ROYALTIES The prescribed fee or gross ticket sales percentage paid to a playwright, producer or director, for the performing rights to a certain play.

RUN The number of performances, or length in terms of weeks or months, for any given show.

RUNNING GAG Comic moment that is repeated throughout a musical or comedy.

RUN-THROUGH A specific rehearsal in which the actors perform long sections of the play (one act or the entire play) without interruption (typically, the director and stage manager take notes and then discuss these with the cast after the rehearsal). Since many rehearsals involve individual scenes, and not the entire cast, the run-through is a way to reassemble all the components and get a sense of the play as a complete unit.

SATIRE Type of play that pokes fun at human beings, our quirks and customs, beliefs and religions, and vices, mostly in a light-hearted vein.

SCENARIO Outline of the play.

SCENE Division of an ACT, usually denoting a change in time or place; can also describe the physical location of a play.

SCENE BREAKDOWN A list of the scenes, noting which characters are in which scenes; sometimes includes costume and set changes.

SCHTICK A repeated bit of comic business, routine, or gimmick used by a performer.

SCRIM A loosely woven cotton or linen fabric (traditionally; modern scrims can be made of gauze or netting) made into a curtain, flat, drop or set that appears opaque when lit from the front, but becomes transparent when lit from behind.

SCRIPT The result of the writings of the PLAYWRIGHT, including dialogue, lyrics, settings, and stage directions for a play or musical.

SET The complete stage setting for a SCENE, ACT, or play.

SET DESIGNER (see also DESIGNER) Member of the artistic team who works with the director to create the sets that will create the overall look of the production. He or she will design backdrops, props, furniture and other elements that make up the physical settings and/or scenes of the play. Most set designers also handle costume design to ensure a consistent look for the production.

SET DRESSING / DECORATING The art of decorating the set with objects and accessories that complete the look, but may have no actual function; they help set the overall tone and mood of the scene.

SIGHT GAG Visual humor derived from a funny prop, costume, make-up, hairstyle or action.

SIGHT LINES Imaginary lines drawn from any given seats in the HOUSE to the stage; these determine what parts of the stage will be visible to audience members sitting in those seats.

SITE-SPECIFIC THEATER This falls into two sub-categories. One type is, for example, a play about a pastor in a church that is actually staged in a church; the other is using, for instance, a swimming pool as a stage for a play, but not necessarily one that is about swimming. Trees, entire towns, courts of law and all sorts of other non-theater locations have been used to stage site-specific plays.

SLAPSTICK Physical comedy that uses horseplay and buffoonery, often with a lot of physical contact between the performers.

SLOW BURN Slow comic realization that something bad has happened; the disgust and anger builds within the actor until she or he explodes in rage.

SLOW TAKE When an actor slowly looks out to the audience as he or she slowly realizes what has been said or done on the stage.

SOLILOQUY Revealing inner thoughts of a character, spoken alone on stage. Often lyrical and highly emotional. An example is Hamlet's "to be, or not to be."

SOUND DESIGNER Works in close collaboration with the COMPOSER to create the overall sound style of the play. He or she may opt for a classical sound or a sharp, modern tone. The sound designer often records music or sound effects that are used in the creation of environmental situations and the general sense of scene.

STAGE The part of the theater where shows are performed. See also PROSCENIUM ARCH and THRUST STAGE.

STAGE DOOR The backstage entrance where the cast and crew enter and exit the theater.

STAGE LEFT / STAGE RIGHT The left or right side of the stage from the actors' point of view. For example, for an actor, the stage left area would be the area on his or her left, but would be the right side of the stage from the perspective of the audience.

STAGE CREW / STAGEHANDS The crew that works backstage during a show, shifting scenery, moving props, etc.

STAGE MANAGER Member of a theater company who accepts full responsibility for the running of a show once it has passed opening night; the stage manager effectively takes over from the director at this point. The stage manager "calls the show" (gives the commands to execute all cues during performance), ensures the actors are present and ready, and that all components of the show are in order.

STAGED READING / WORKSHOP Usually done with new plays that have yet to be produced. A public performance of a play-in-progress in which actors read from scripts and sometimes include simple actions; no sets, props or costumes are involved. The purpose of this is to enable the PLAYWRIGHT, and if one is involved, the DRAMATURG, to "hear" what has been, until then, words written on paper. A workshop is commonly done before a new play receives its first full production.

STAND-BY An actor hired to fill in regular slots when the main actor has scheduled days off. This is sometimes done to comply with actors' union regulations that limit the number of performances per week to eight; where the show is scheduled for more than eight, the stand-by will be brought in.

STEAL A SCENE When an actor attracts attention that should be focused on another actor. Children and animals have always been notorious "scene stealers."

STRAIGHT MAN An actor who delivers non-comedic lines (straight lines) to a comic, helping set up jokes.

STREET THEATER Open-air spaces, commonly in large public places, where acting troupes try to attract audiences, often for the purpose of social activism.

STRIKE To remove or "tear-down," usually a SET. But can also include the removal of a prop. After a production closes, the entire set and props are "struck."

SUBTEXT The unspoken words that hide behind the spoken line. Sometimes the PLAYWRIGHT purposely denotes subtext in the stage directions; other times the actors, with input from the director, invent the subtext appropriate to their characters and situations. This helps achieve the sense of immediate truth.

SWING Singer and/or dancer who is prepared to step in for a chorus member who is unable to perform.

TABLEAU Moment in which a living picture is created on the stage and held by the actors without motion or speech.

TAG LINE Final line of a SCENE or ACT, or the exit line of any major character. When it is the final line of an ACT it is also called the "curtain line."

TECHNICAL REHEARSAL First rehearsal in which technical elements, such as lights, sets, and sound, are combined with the performances of the actors.

TEXT Words of the dialogue, and lyrics.

THEATER CRITIC Someone whose written reaction to and opinion of the theater production is published with the intention of enriching the theater experience for others who might attend. The theater critic normally publishes his or her criticism in a newspaper or magazine article.

THEME The central idea or thought of a play that establishes a common ground for the audience.

THESPIAN Another, more traditional, word for ACTOR.

THROW-AWAY The underplaying of a moment in a SCENE.

THRUST STAGE This is a type of stage layout (see also PROSCENIUM ARCH), and is most often used by classical Shakespearean companies. The thrust stage is set a bit higher than the first rows of audience seating and cuts directly into the house. The audience sits around the stage, sometimes in a curved format, and sometimes angled on all three sides of the stage.

TIMING Knowing when the exact right moment comes to speak a line or perform an action for maximum effect. See also PACING.

TRAGEDY Type of play that deals with sorrow and human suffering.

TYPECASTING Selection of actors based upon their physical similarity to a certain dramatic type, or on their reputation for specializing in a specific kind of role.

UNDERSTUDY An actor who has rehearsed the role of another actor so that she or he can fill in should the other actor be unable to perform; usually happens in an emergency situation due to injury or illness. The understudy is often another member of the same cast. The understudy also understudies the STAND-BY.

UPSTAGE Area of the stage farthest from the audience. Also, when an actor draws attention to him or herself, inappropriately taking the attention away from the other actors.

USHERS Members of the FRONT-OF-HOUSE (FOH) staff who guide audience members to their seats, and often remain in the auditorium during performances in case of emergency.

WALK-ON A small acting role with no lines.

WINGS Offstage areas to the right and left of the STAGE or PLAYING SPACE.